CREATING THE
ONE-SHOT
LIBRARY WORKSHOP
A Step-by-Step Guide

JERILYN VELDOF

American Library Association
Chicago   2006

While extensive effort has gone into ensuring the reliability of information appearing in this book, the publisher makes no warranty, express or implied, on the accuracy or reliability of the information, and does not assume and hereby disclaims any liability to any person for any loss or damage caused by errors or omissions in this publication.

Composition by ALA Editions in Helvetica and Electra using QuarkXPress 5.0 on a PC platform

Printed on 50-pound white offset, a pH-neutral stock, and bound in 10-point coated cover stock by Data Reproductions

The paper used in this publication meets the minimum requirements of American National Standard for Information Sciences—Permanence of Paper for Printed Library Materials, ANSI Z39.48-1992. ∞

Library of Congress Cataloging-in-Publication Data

Veldof, Jerilyn R.
  Creating the one-shot library workshop : a step-by-step guide / Jerilyn Veldof.
    p.   cm.
  Includes bibliographical references and index.
  ISBN 0-8389-0913-2
  1. Library orientation. 2. Library institutes and workshops. I. Title.
  Z711.2.V46 2006
  025.5'6—dc22   2005033222

Printed in the United States of America

10 09 08 07 06   5 4 3 2 1

To my mother,
the first librarian in the family

Contents

Acknowledgments

This book would not have been possible if it were not for the many wonderful colleagues I have worked with at the University of Minnesota who have contributed to many rounds of this instructional design process for the "Unravel the Library" workshop series. Their willingness to embark on this process has helped me take my learning from books and workshops into the field. And in working with a team of dedicated and passionate educators I have learned far more than I ever could have alone. I especially want to thank the core group of designers who have kept coming back on a volunteer basis over the last five years of design cycles: Lynne Beck, Malaika Grant, Van Houlson, Kimberly Clarke, Melissa Kalpin Prescott, and Debra Payne Chaparro.

In addition to the contributions of our library staff, I leaned on the input of several colleagues outside of the University of Minnesota Libraries. A big thank-you to Lisa Janicke Hinchliffe (University of Illinois Library at Urbana-Champaign) for rising above the call of duty and providing meticulous feedback on an early draft. Ruth Dickstein (University of Arizona) and Scott Walters (University of Kansas) provided valuable insights on various chapters; and a former professor of mine, Barry Johansen in Human Resource Development at the University of Minnesota, was helpful in steering the initial chapters of the book.

Thanks also to my mother, Marilyn Veldof, who provided grammatical guidance on every sentence of my initial drafts (as she has on everything I've ever published). My childhood best friend, Erik Pyontek, volunteered his creative talents to design illustrations for the manuscript. Last but not least my partner, Anna Anderhagen, very graciously helped me free up my weekends and nights to work on this manuscript. Thanks so much to you all!

Introduction

Good instruction should not be left to chance and luck. Most of us in libraries get a very limited amount of time with our learners. Even though we might be making some breakthroughs in certain areas to infuse information literacy into the curriculum or the communities with which we work, these tend to be the exceptions, not the rule. Most libraries still have to live with the fifty-minute workshop, the one-shot stand-up routine where we are expected to teach learners everything they need to know. It's a far, far cry from the ideal, but "fifty minutes is better than nothing," we say and bravely go into that lab or classroom with the hope that we might be able to make some kind of difference. And who knows, a number of exceptional fifty-minute workshops sewn together may begin to build an instruction program. A strong instruction program that makes a difference in the learning and performance of our learners may help us develop the partnerships we need to build a true information literacy program.

> *One thing about the instructional design process that's bizarre is that most of us like to start with thinking about how somebody is going to learn something. We would never write down objectives or do a task analysis because we already have it down in our minds. We think we understand the tasks that go into a particular skill. We just assume.*
>
> —Van Houlson, Business Librarian,
> University of Minnesota Libraries–Twin Cities

Every minute, therefore, that we have with our learners in the one-shot workshop needs to be intentionally designed to increase learning and performance. How can we best accomplish this? By building our understanding about teaching and learning and by using a process to implement that understanding.

This book is intended to provide you with a deliberate process of instructional design and the essential background information to help ensure the resounding success of your library workshops. The process described in this book is best suited for those workshops that you teach frequently or that are taught by more than one librarian. Having said that, however, aspects of the process can be easily adapted into the development of unique or infrequently offered workshops as well.

Tip

What's a "one-shot" library workshop? It's a task-focused training session. A one-shot, for example, might focus on helping library users find a book in the catalog, locate primary source material, or evaluate websites. The library instructor's main contact with the learners generally begins and ends with the one-shot workshop.

INTRODUCTION TO THE INSTRUCTIONAL DESIGN PROCESS

Take a moment to reflect on how you personally learned to plan in-class time as an instructor. Did you have a course in college or in graduate school? Did you go to development workshops on this topic?

Part of the problem faced by instruction librarians and staff is that few of us have ever learned effective instructional design. For those who have, much of it may have been focused on the delivery of the information, not on the design of the workshop. We may have learned some presentation techniques or learning theory, but unfortunately it's very uncommon to have actually learned how to design a workshop from beginning to end.

Take a moment to reflect on the ways you design your workshops. Do you

_____ Make an outline of content areas you'd like to cover?

_____ Have students ask you questions and then answer them as a way to shape your workshop time?

_____ Include a lecture and demonstration followed by hands-on time when the students can try it out for themselves?

_____ Use a colleague's outline on what to cover and then "wing it" when you get into the classroom or lab?

_____ Create a worksheet of exercises for the learners to work through during the session and build the workshop around these exercises?

_____ What else? _____

This list is fairly typical of what I hear in my instructional design workshops when I ask participants how they design their own workshops. Some participants say they may use one or two of these approaches most often and mix and match many of the others depending on a variety of factors.

But you might want to think about building a workshop as a process that looks more like that of building a house. If the builder skips the foundation, he might be able to build something that stands for a while, but only for a while. If the builder then decides that what he really likes are kitchens and spends most of the time building the kitchen at the expense of the other rooms, the rest of the house will reflect that choice. And if he throws on a cheap roof because he went over budget, eventually the roof will start leaking.

It's the same kind of thing when designing a library workshop. You could choose to focus on the content and end up pulling together the teaching methods at the last minute or even on the spot. You could decide to focus on just the section of the workshop you really enjoy, and gloss over the rest. Alternatively, you could follow a blueprint for the design that takes the mystery out of what seems like an elusive process—the design of a library workshop—and gives it structure and predictability.

Next we'll look at the instructional design model used in this book.

OVERVIEW OF INSTRUCTIONAL DESIGN

The most widely used and respected instructional design methodology used in the training field is called instructional systems design, or ISD. For the most part, ISD is basically the application of educational psychology to teaching, development, and delivery. Training professionals are schooled in it, and it is the standard for training departments in companies around the world.

Instructional systems design methodology is a systematic approach to designing training that applies to many different learning environments. It includes analysis, design, development, implementation, and evaluation. These stages in the design process are often referred to by the acronym ADDIE. There are numerous adaptations of the ISD ADDIE model in the training and education field (including models from Irwin Goldstein, Dugan Laird, Richard Swanson, Walter Dick and Lou Carey, Frederick Knirk and Kent Gustafson, John Campbell, and Richard Johnson). The ISD version used in this book comes largely from the self-proclaimed largest train-the-trainer company in the world, Langevin Learning Services (http://www.langevin.com).

In order to give a big-picture look at the design process described in this book, figure 1-1 breaks down the ISD process into the five "ADDIE" components which are explained in the next section.

THE PROCESS

1. Analysis

The instructional design process starts as any good process does—with background work. The designer investigates the needs of the agency or person who is either contracting the session or who might encourage or require learners to attend the session, if applicable. Then they turn to the needs, situation, and abilities of the expected learners in the workshop.

2. Design

Once this background work has been done, the focus changes to what content will be covered. Using a rather rigorous and complete process, the instructional designer identifies these content areas down to the very specifics. Objectives for the workshop are articulated during this part of the design, as are the ways the instructor will be able to check that these objectives are being met.

FIGURE 1-1   Instructional Design Cycle

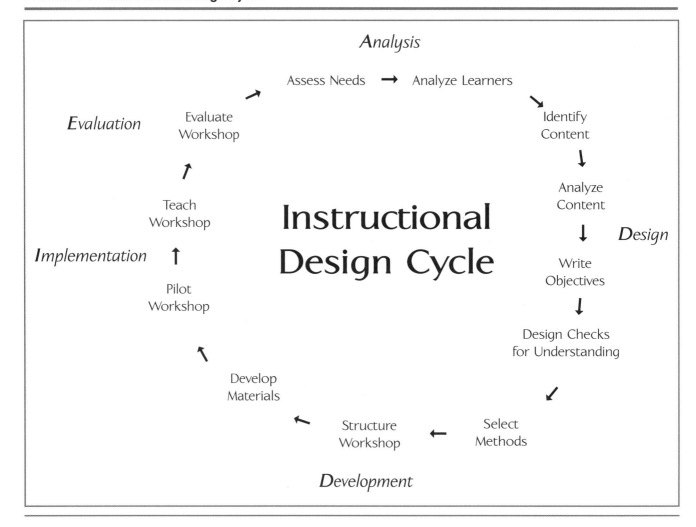

It is only then that the focus moves to *how* these objectives will be met. Teaching methods that fit the learner analysis completed earlier in the process and that complement the content are chosen and designed for the workshop.

3. Development

Then these methods are shaped into a workable lesson plan and other logistics are developed, such as instructor and learner materials.

4. Implementation

The workshop is tested and revised and is then officially offered and taught by the library.

5. Evaluation

Finally, evaluation feedback is analyzed and the designer decides if a redesign process is merited for the next time the workshop is offered.

WHY GO THROUGH ALL THIS?

At this point you may be looking at all these parts of the design process and flipping through this book thinking, "This is crazy! I'll never have enough time to do all this!" And for most of us, that is very true. Every designer will have to weigh time costs against benefits and decide what part of the process they will focus on and what parts they can hasten through or even skip over. (See the section "Allotting Time and Money for the Process" in the next chapter to help you decide what projects and under what circumstances you might choose to move into a more "rapid" design process.) There are many reasons to dive into this process. Here are a few of the ones I have found most compelling.

> ### Tip
>
> As instruction librarians we sometimes end up teaching content in the classroom or lab that should be addressed at the library's website or in the physical library. Yes, we can create a fantastic segment in our workshops on finding appropriate indexes on the library's website, but shouldn't the website do that adequately? Do we need to outline and expand on the research and writing process if we can make an online tool that does just that? Instead of "fixing" what's wrong when you get into the classroom, fix and improve as much of the problem as you can outside the classroom. This will free up your class time for instruction in higher-order information literacy skills.

Top Seven Reasons to Use This Design Process

1. Long-Term Use

This design process gives the library an effective in-depth lesson plan that offers consistent content and teaching methods that can be delivered by multiple library instructors year after year.

2. Plug-and-Play Content

This process provides modules that instructors can insert into other workshops, thereby reducing instructional preparation time and individual design. Handouts and worksheets are already created and can be easily customized.

3. Stakeholder Input

This process allows a group of self-identified library stakeholders to take part in deciding the content of the library curriculum.

4. Consistency

This process ensures consistent content and delivery for each individual workshop. You will be able to promise your constituents the same outcomes for each session offered.

5. Training for New Instructors

This process provides a very clear lesson plan that includes objectives, teaching points, activities, worksheets, and instructor guides. This offers apprentice instructors an opportunity to focus on delivery instead of design.

6. Development for Existing Instructors

This process provides an opportunity for library instructors to try some new ways of teaching that have already undergone trial and testing and are deemed successful.

7. Quality

This process creates a high-quality, effective workshop that can be used with confidence over and over again.

OVERVIEW OF THIS BOOK

Now that you are hopefully convinced that trying out this process is a worthwhile endeavor, here is what is in store for you in this book. You will notice that instead of using the five components from the ADDIE model, I have broken down the process even further into more discrete steps. Each chapter covers one step in the process and includes only the most essential background information needed to complete the step. The intent is not to include everything that could be known about the topic, but rather just enough information for you to be successful.

At the end of each chapter, however, I've included a section that explores how the chapter content has played out in "real life" in the library where I work. It is my hope that these case studies will help you begin thinking about how to move from the theory and process discussed in each chapter to application in your own library.

Before moving directly into the process I have included the next chapter, called "Getting Started," which addresses some of the decisions you will need to make before embarking on your design journey. Good luck! May your trail be clear and the wind at your back!

> **Tip**
>
> Although this book has some theory, it mostly focuses on the *process* of design. If you are looking for more theory to supplement the process, check out Walter Dick and Lou Carey's *The Systematic Design of Instruction* (HarperCollins, 1990). Another standard in the field is William Rothwell and H. C. Kazanas's *Mastering the Instructional Design Process* (Jossey-Bass, 1992). If you are looking for lighter fare, try George M. Piskurich's *Rapid Instructional Design: Learning ID Fast and Right* (Jossey-Bass/Pfeiffer, 2000).

SUMMARY

Most librarians are not trained in instructional design, even though effective instructional design can help librarians and staff have an even greater impact on their patrons. This book follows an ISD (instructional systems design) model that breaks the process down into five major parts that follow the acronym ADDIE (analyze, design, develop, implement, evaluate). These parts are broken even further into the steps used in this book.

A kind of teaching fatigue, coupled with extreme staffing shortages and many more instructional requests on campus than could be handled, motivated the University of Minnesota Libraries staff to use their preparation and class time more effectively. As a kickoff, a core group of librarians participated in a day-long training on instructional design. Upon their return they began to put their learning into practice as members of design teams focused on creating one workshop per team.

The products of these design teams are a series of "Unravel the Library" workshops that are designed to meet the often overwhelming need for library instruction generated by over seventy sections of English Composition each semester. English Composition instructors and other instructors in targeted departments send their students to these workshops either as a requirement or for extra credit. Students are directed to sign up for a session that fits into their schedules, and upon completion of the workshop they are given a certificate of completion as proof of attendance.

Because the workshops were designed by key stakeholders in the library and because the lesson plan is very detailed, we are able to distribute the teaching responsibility to about fifteen library staff instructors who teach over 100 sessions of the workshops each semester. These instructors are recruited from the entire library (librarians and non-librarians), including shelving, processing, and special collections staff. New recruits go through a standardized training process that includes a training session, observation, assisting, and then finally full teaching responsibilities. The instructors teach from a detailed lesson plan, and all of their handouts and worksheets are duplicated and made available for them.

Librarians who teach one-shot class sessions for specific faculty can choose to adapt a section or more of the Unravel workshops into their own sessions. Access to the handouts and lesson plans is available on the Web for them to customize relevant sections in a way that will work for their disciplines and instructional objectives.

The Unravel the Library workshop series consists of three workshops:

Unravel the Library 1: Orientation and Tour

Unravel the Library 2: The Research Process (the central
    workshop for English Composition)

Unravel the Library 3: Advanced Searching

A fourth workshop, Unravel the Library for Grads, was offered for several years and subsequently dropped from the series due to the increasing availability of alternative discipline-centered workshops offered by individual librarians.

These workshops will be discussed in some depth in subsequent case study sections in each chapter.

Getting Started

Before jumping in and getting started, there are a number of things to think about first. Will you work alone or with others? How much time should you allocate to the process? What instructional design skills do you lack? Do you need to find funding to help you with the process? The first of these questions to address is whether you will work alone or with others.

USING TEAMS, PARTNERS, OR DESIGNING INDEPENDENTLY

The four main ways to follow the design process are

- Individually
- Individually with a sounding board
- With a partner
- In a team

Let's look at each one of these separately.

Individual Design

In many libraries, the librarian in charge of a discipline or subject library is the only person who selects materials, works with the patrons interested in that area (and the faculty and students if in an academic library), and delivers the discipline's library instruction. The librarian may adapt someone else's outline and incorporate other people's teaching methods learned while assisting them, but more frequently than not, workshops are designed and taught as a solo venture. In many libraries there often is not the luxury of adequate staffing to work in any other way. Whether culturally or pragmatically driven, solo design may be the most feasible way to design your workshops.

Even in situations where a collaborative design approach is a possibility, solo design may be the most comfortable way to begin. This approach might give you the leeway to take some risks and to experiment without worrying about what colleagues are thinking. The solo design approach may also allow you to question some of your assumptions about teaching and learning and "the way you've always done it," but on your own time schedule and intensity. If this sounds like what you need, then try the design process as a solo venture.

Individual Design with a Sounding Board

Although many library staff are not in a position to collaborate on workshop designs, there may be colleagues who would be willing to act as sounding boards as you develop a workshop. Sounding boards are people available to discuss your ideas and give you some feedback. If none of your library's staff are available, you may want to find someone in a similar library at the local level, or even regionally or nationally if you agree to work online or via the phone.

As you finish each step in the design process, pass this to your sounding board for comments. Since the role of the sounding board is to challenge you in the process, choose someone who would be willing to ask, "Why are you doing x? Why did you choose to do y? What about z?" But be careful not to get defensive. Remember, you don't want to choose someone who says, "Oh, this is great," but someone who is able to give you substantive feedback and ask difficult questions.

It may be even more useful to team up with a librarian who is designing his or her own workshop and act as sounding boards to each other. This is a great way to learn from each other. One person, for example, might choose a particular teaching method to use, while the other person chooses something very different. During the evaluation step the pair can discuss and compare teaching methods, perhaps using the other's methods the next time the workshop is offered.

Partner Design

The natural progression from designing individually with a sounding board is to invite your "sounding board" to design a workshop together with you—or even just one common segment of a workshop. For example, if you are the business librarian and often teach a segment on a ProQuest database, and you know that your colleague who is the sociology librarian also teaches a ProQuest database, you might collaborate to codesign this segment of your workshops. Likewise, it might be possible to enlist a cohort at another library system to partner with you on a workshop design that you will both teach in the separate libraries. Partnering on the online catalog segment of the workshop, for example, may be a natural connection you have with other instruction librarians both within your system and with those who use the same vendor in other libraries.

Team Design

The next level of design is with a group of people who are working on delivering either the same segments of a workshop (e.g., the OPAC) or the entire workshop (e.g., an orientation to the library). This may be the best way to provide a common workshop that is frequently offered and taught by a number of librarians. The team approach has many benefits over the individual or partner approach. Pulling together a diverse team of reference/instruction librarians, subject bibliographers, computer programmers and web designers, library staff from processing units, and catalogers with various teaching experience and generational backgrounds can

Create a healthy level of debate and conflict around what we should be teaching and how

Encourage a blending of your traditional content with more cutting-edge content (which may not have been included otherwise)

Push the team beyond the usual comfort levels and propose unique, creative approaches to teaching

Provide an entire team of instructors, rovers, and observers to evaluate the workshop

Result in a very well thought-out and informed workshop design

- The way I'm reading it, east is the shortest route.
- Your map's wrong! West is the quickest way to get there!

Provide the design team and others with workshop materials they can adapt and use and reuse in their individual instruction sessions

In addition to all these benefits, user education coordinators and heads of instruction will be interested in the use of the team design process to speed up the diffusion of design skills and of teaching competencies throughout the library. For each design process, groups of librarians and staff learn the instructional design process by actually doing it—creating a product that will be used multiple times by the library. The skills they learn can be applied to designing future workshops in their subject areas or collaboratively across disciplines. Furthermore, librarians who have never wavered from the lecture–demo–hands-on teaching formula have access to lesson plans with creative and fun teaching methods that they can practice, thus building confidence and teaching skills.

Team Challenges

Although the benefits of team design are many, working with a diverse group of designers brings its own challenges. You will need to think about the team's makeup and dynamics, and you will need to know something about project management and team development to make sure this is a successful venture.

> **Tip**
>
> For information about running meetings effectively, see John E. Tropman's book *Making Meetings Work: Achieving High Quality Group Decisions* (Sage, 2003).

Building the Team

The first step is to choose team members wisely. Look for a group of anywhere from three to eight people who are the following:

A mix of "subject matter experts" (also called SMEs)

Find staff who work in different areas of the library—cataloging, shelving, circulation, information technology, reference, instruction, orientation, and so on—and include a volunteer or staff member who would be part of the target audience if possible, such as an undergraduate or a senior citizen if that is your target. At some point in the design process, each member will be able to offer his or her unique expertise to the process.

A mix of personality types

Find the renegade experimentalists who will question the status quo and rock the boat, but also seek out the placaters and soothers who will keep the meetings from erupting too much. Find very creative people and very structured people. Find big-picture thinkers and sequential thinkers. During the design phase, each member will be able to bring different strengths (and enthusiasm) to each one of the steps.

A mix of learning styles

Find design members who represent all types of learners (as explained in step 2). You will want, for example, to have people on the team who are "activists" and "pragmatists," but also those who are considered "reflectors" and "theorists." Include visual learners as well as kinesthetic and auditory learners. These team members will help ensure that there are pieces of the workshop design that fit their specific learning style preferences.

A mix of status

Be sure to find a member or two who will add legitimacy to the design, such as a senior member of the staff or the coordinator of instruction. This team may also be your opportunity to mentor a new librarian into the teaching and designing process, so don't overlook the novice instructor. Be wary, however, when there are people on the team who outrank each other or who have some kind of power (explicit or implicit) over another. This will change the team dynamics, and you may have to work harder at creating a safe space for dissension and open discussion.

Stages of Team Growth

Now that the team is in place, the next step is to address team dynamics. It can be a sizable challenge to get the new team to gel and work together productively and efficiently in what is probably a short timeline. Teams generally go through four stages before they are performing at their peak. The more smoothly and quickly you can facilitate the team through these stages, the faster you will get your work done.

Stage 1: Forming

At this stage individuals in the newly formed team will begin to get a sense of where they stand in the group and what they can contribute. But they may also be suspicious of the task ("Do we really have to go through this whole thing just to teach a workshop?") and perhaps be confused and somewhat reticent about the process ("I've been teaching for years and I've never done this whole process; will I look stupid in front of my more junior colleagues?"). Discussions can swing widely from lofty concepts and issues to what may seem like tangential minutiae. The team might be easily distracted and little work gets done here.

Stage 2: Storming

By now in the process, members are wondering if they've gotten in over their heads—or made a terrible mistake in becoming part of the team. Ways they have thought about teaching and their areas of expertise are being questioned at the foundational level. Their confidence can begin to shake. Team members will argue, get frustrated, become defensive, and factions may start to form (e.g., the "We *must* teach Boolean" faction up against the "Boolean is dead and forget it" faction). The team is going in a million different directions and it seems impossible that a workshop could emerge from this dissension and chaos. Depending on how conflict-avoidant the team is, members may need to be reminded during this stage that airing conflicting opinions is an important part of the work of the team because it will make the final workshop much more effective. The team facilitator should watch for those members who shut down and disengage from the process at this stage. They may need careful coaxing and support to express their views.

Stage 3: Norming

In this next stage team members have finally acclimated to each other and to the process. They realize that eventually they have got to stop the craziness and actually get the workshop designed. They become more cooperative, more accepting of conflicting opinions, and are able to address their issues more constructively. The team will feel more comfortable with each other personally as well—maybe even chummy.

Stage 4: Performing

Finally, in stage 4, the team will be making significant progress. It's possible that at this point the team will scrap all the work done previously and start over, much more efficiently this time. Or it's possible that the team continues in the direction they have been working on, but significantly revising previous work. If the majority of this team next turns to a new workshop design, the process will go remarkably faster, since the team will have already learned to "perform" together.

Ongoing Cycles

The pacing of these cycles can vary depending on the team's dynamics. Expect to move through these stages in anywhere from one or two meetings to months of meeting together. The cost of an elongated process is that the team can become very frustrated and possibly disengaged as they distance themselves from the debate and from possible criticism of "the way they've always done it." One problem to watch out for is that team members' feelings might become directed at the instructional design process itself, instead of the team's own dynamics. If instructional design is going to catch on in your library and become a positive and integral part of your work, it's important to carefully attend to team dynamics prior to the performing stage.

Dealing with Your Team Prior to Stage 4

If possible, enlist a facilitator who is not part of the design process or who is taking a secondary role in the process. The facilitator should pay particular attention to team dynamics, watching for members who may be shutting down in the meetings, and others who are taking the floor disproportionately or fighting "unfairly." The facilitator may need to intervene more frequently in the early stages of team formation in order to help move the team along.

Have small segments of the design process accomplished in subteams. If there are factions within the team, make sure each side is represented on the subteam so the other faction does not discount their work.

Use subteams to "experiment" with different possibilities as a way to respond to conflicting opinions or factions in the team.

Make the team stage process discussed above visible to the team. Talk about the stages and emphasize the importance of each stage.

> *Tip*
>
> For a great book on leading teams, see Peter R. Scholtes's *The Team Handbook: How to Use Teams to Improve Quality* (Joiner, 1998). It includes a number of tools to help the team over difficult spots and elaborates on the four stages of team growth discussed earlier.

ALLOTTING TIME AND MONEY FOR THE PROCESS

Time

How much time should you allot to an instructional design process? Of course, the answer is, "it depends." The metric below can help you assess this question. Respond to each of the questions with a numerical ranking. The higher the ranking, the more staff and time might be allocated to the process.

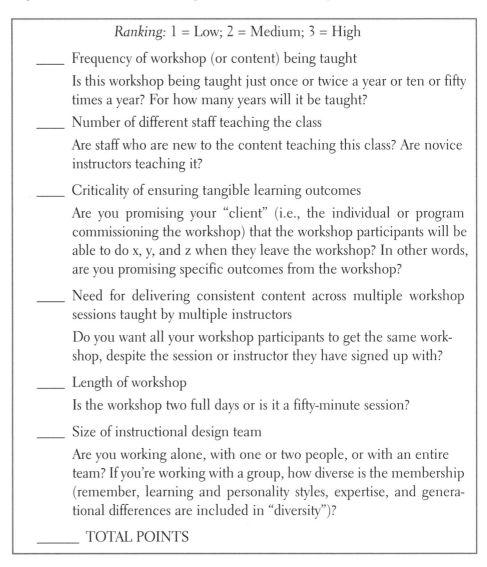

Ranking: 1 = Low; 2 = Medium; 3 = High

____ Frequency of workshop (or content) being taught

Is this workshop being taught just once or twice a year or ten or fifty times a year? For how many years will it be taught?

____ Number of different staff teaching the class

Are staff who are new to the content teaching this class? Are novice instructors teaching it?

____ Criticality of ensuring tangible learning outcomes

Are you promising your "client" (i.e., the individual or program commissioning the workshop) that the workshop participants will be able to do x, y, and z when they leave the workshop? In other words, are you promising specific outcomes from the workshop?

____ Need for delivering consistent content across multiple workshop sessions taught by multiple instructors

Do you want all your workshop participants to get the same workshop, despite the session or instructor they have signed up with?

____ Length of workshop

Is the workshop two full days or is it a fifty-minute session?

____ Size of instructional design team

Are you working alone, with one or two people, or with an entire team? If you're working with a group, how diverse is the membership (remember, learning and personality styles, expertise, and generational differences are included in "diversity")?

_____ TOTAL POINTS

The higher the score (12–18 points), the more time will be needed to design this particular workshop. You decide how much that is: would 5 meetings that are 2 hours in length represent a significant time investment? Or would that look more like 15 meetings that are 2 hours each? More?

A score under 6 points indicates that it is probably not worth spending too much time designing this workshop. You decide how much that is: 3 hours? 6 hours? 12 hours?

These factors, of course, need to be weighed against the very real time and staffing pressures that most librarians experience.

The next thing to consider is the options for first-time use of the design process:

1. Follow the entire design process for just one segment of a workshop.

   Example: Design a 15–20 minute section on the OPAC using this process and then follow your traditional design process for the rest of the workshop.

2. Select only a few steps to start with.

   Perhaps you decide to use the design steps that you normally skip in your personal design process, or those that might challenge you to think about your content and your teaching in a different way. The rest of the process you would follow might be the "way you've always done it."

Once you have used the steps for one segment, or used a selected number of steps for the whole workshop, you will have a better idea of the time needed for the entire process. Each of the steps can be done with varying degrees of thoroughness. Decide ahead how many meetings or hours you will allot to the design process and discuss the level of thoroughness you'd like to apply for each step.

If you are designing the workshop alone, you might plan to complete a number of steps in one sitting. As you add people to the process, however, you will need to plan for extra time—each additional person means that much more time for opinions, perspectives, and overall discussion.

Design experience will also play a part. Novice groups will need additional time to work through the process. The first instructional design team at the University of Minnesota met as many as twenty times to design our first workshop from beginning to end, evaluate it, and make changes. Subsequent designs thankfully took far less time. The time you invest up front, however, will pay off in many ways to the library. The University of Minnesota's Unravel workshops, for example, not only have helped train over a dozen library "instructional designers," but they bring in over 1,400 students each year to high-quality, interesting workshops. And once a workshop has been designed, subsequent redesigns and tweaking take far less time. These workshops can then be offered again and again for many years with no more design necessary, and they come with an in-depth, well-written lesson plan that can be used by multiple instructors.

The blank worksheet found in the appendix can be used to designate a rough time schedule for each step.

Money

It may be wise at the onset of the design process to begin securing some funds that could be used to provide incentives for participation during the assessment stage, the workshop pilot, and the final evaluation. This might include funds to

> *You have to leave a lot more time than you think. From beginning to end, to really follow the whole process takes a lot longer than you think, especially when working with a group. But you don't actually have to follow all the steps of the process for it to be useful. And even just asking that first question of yourself and the instructors you work with—the one about what the students need to know to be successful—that really does change things.*
>
> —Malaika Grant, Reference and Instruction Librarian, University of Minnesota Libraries–Twin Cities

Pay people to participate in focus groups or interviews during the assessment step of the design process

Buy pizza or lunches to entice people to come to a focus group or interview

Pay people to come to a pilot test and stay to help evaluate it

Encourage a client to help design and administer an evaluation of the learners' paper, presentation, or other such product (See step 1 for a discussion of clients.)

How much money to pay someone to participate in a focus group or pilot varies greatly with the participant and the location. For college students in the Twin Cities area, for example, I have found that competition for their time is fierce enough that offering pizza and pop is not an adequate enticement. Students will generally preregister and actually show up at a specific time and place for about fifteen dollars an hour, but when recruited on the spot (at the student union, for example, while they're hanging out between classes), many can be enticed for as little as ten dollars an hour with cookies and soda. Faculty will usually show up for just a free lunch or dinner, along with an inner sense of obligation or gratitude to the library. To find out what works for your participant group, ask a few representative members of the group and then give it a try. If that doesn't work, increase the amount of the incentive until you have reached that "sweet spot."

For some, a discussion about money needs to go beyond the cost of incentives. If you come from a library where you have to complete a cost-benefit analysis to show a return on investment (ROI) for your workshop, there is an informative section on creating a "quick and dirty" analysis in George M. Piskurich's book *Rapid Instructional Design: Learning ID Fast and Right* (Jossey-Bass/Pfeiffer, 2000).

After thinking about and resolving these issues, you should now be ready to jump into the design process.

SUMMARY

There are four main ways to design a workshop: by yourself, with a sounding board, with a partner, or as part of a team. If you are building a team, look for a mix of subject matter experts with a diversity of personality types and learning styles. Then facilitate the group through the forming, storming, norming, and performing stages of team development.

There are many factors that contribute to a decision about how much time should be allocated to the design process. These include the frequency the workshop will be offered, the number of different staff who might teach the workshop, how essential it is that learning outcomes be met, and how consistent the different offerings of the workshop need to be.

The last consideration to make before starting is whether funds may be needed to pay for incentives for attendance at focus groups, interviews, or pilot workshops.

Many of the public service and liaison librarians at the University of Minnesota Libraries were invested in the effective and successful library instruction of the first year required English Composition courses. In some ways, this contact with students might be the most critical— or the only—instruction opportunity the library has. It therefore made sense that a number of stakeholders would group together to make sure that this contact was the most valuable use of our time possible.

Design teams of approximately six to eight librarians and staff were formed initially and met over a two- to five-month period to design each of the Unravel the Library workshops. The design teams then reconvened to evaluate the pilot test and redesign and refine sections of the workshops where necessary.

Because of the critical role of these workshops for first-year English Composition students, the design team followed the entire design process for the first run-through. Most of the subsequent redesigns focused on one section of the workshops at a time and involved following only the steps in the process that needed revision.

Each of the workshops entailed a different amount of up-front design time. In contrast to all the work put into Unravel 2: The Research Process, the workshop that precedes this one in the Unravel series (Unravel 1: Orientation and Tour) has only undergone one full design process and only a few small revisions. It is a tour and orientation to the libraries and needed much less work than the other workshops we have designed.

Unravel 3: Advanced Searching is basically a spinoff of Unravel 2 and includes content that could not be included in that workshop. This meant that the design segment of the design process went very quickly and the team was able to focus more on the other parts of the design process.

The last workshop, Unravel for Grads, went through three quick design cycles. It was built with the prerequisite that students would either have attended the previous Unravels or already have that basic knowledge. Because Unravel for Grads was offered as a stand-alone (not attached to a department, program, or school), voluntary attendance was spotty and there was no need to offer it many times each semester. In addition, more discipline-focused workshops are being offered by subject librarians that are often more helpful for graduates than a generic Unravel workshop is. These forces led the design group to pull the Unravel for Grads offerings and redirect students to these discipline-focused library sessions instead.

Recently the University of Minnesota Libraries have thrown a grenade into the middle of the Unravel workshops. The new federated search engine and two new library portals have necessitated another full-blown workshop design process from start to end. This design project started with a one-day retreat with all self-appointed stakeholders invited. A smaller team of eight librarians spent four months implementing and building upon the ideas and direction of this retreat to redesign the three Unravel workshops.

Are You All Set?

Have you figured out your

- ✔ Design configuration (teams, partners, sounding boards, or solo design)?
- ✔ Timeline?
- ✔ Funds?

Now you are ready to start designing!

STEP 1

Assess Needs

Step 1 is one of the most important steps in the entire instructional design cycle. If you are thinking about cutting corners, please do not start here. Admittedly, there are certainly temptations to do so. This step entails talking to people with whom we may not usually interact. It means asking questions and stepping outside of our expert role to truly listen to what others have to say. And what we hear may call into question our old ways of covering x, y, and z or of approaching instruction. Any one of these things alone may push us out of our comfort zone.

Despite hesitations and concerns, this is too valuable a step to miss. The needs assessment serves as the foundation upon which the whole workshop is built. There is never a shortage of content that can be taught. A good needs assessment tells you which of all that content is the most essential for the learners. Just as important, it helps you figure out what *not* to teach. This is extremely valuable information that is worth its weight in gold—especially if you're looking at fifty or sixty short minutes in front of a class. If you get this wrong and end up teaching nonessential information or take nonessential tangents, you will end up wasting your time and that of your learners.

In order to conduct a needs assessment, first you need to identify the person or group who is creating the need in the first place—in other words, the client.

IDENTIFYING THE CLIENT

In many cases the primary client is clear: it is the person who picked up the phone and asked if you could provide training for their group or class. In other cases it's less clear-cut. What makes a client a client is that he or she

Is the person who wants a group of people to learn something in particular (e.g., a senior citizen group being able to conduct genealogy research on the Web or students in the International Politics course being able to find statistics for their paper)

Is the person who ultimately decides if the people in this group and if the group as a whole are successful (e.g., if after the training the senior citizens are conducting genealogy research on the Web or if the politics students are using statistics in their papers)

Is in a position to require or strongly encourage the group to attend the library workshop

Identifying a Client for "Open" Workshops

Not every workshop a library offers is at the request of a particular client. Often workshops are offered because it makes sense to respond to a widespread instructional need all at once, rather than one-on-one at the desk or in consultation sessions. These are "open" workshops for any participants who choose to attend. They start with a need recognized by library staff. For example:

At the reference desk users seem to be confused about finding books and journals in the catalog.

There seems to be some confusion for new immigrants about how a North American library works, including how to find books on open stacks.

Job seekers continuously come in asking for help doing company research.

> The way that you start is by asking deeper and different questions than you might normally about the learner. The idea of asking what do the students need to know—and using that question when you work with faculty—instead of using "what do you want me to cover" really changes your point of view.
>
> —Malaika Grant, Reference and Instruction Librarian, University of Minnesota Libraries–Twin Cities

In many cases the need reveals itself through a library staff's interaction with users. Often we stop there, and the ensuing workshop is loosely configured around what the users appear to need and what we in the library believe they need to learn. This approach contributes to defining needs and what it means for the learners to be successful in a myopic, library-centered way that limits our ability to be truly effective.

Identifying a client is the first step in moving beyond these limitations. As discussed later in this chapter, a client can help the instructional designer identify the most critical content, learn more about the learner, and eventually market the workshop. In cases where there is not a clear-cut client, as in the scenarios just listed, asking "Why does the learner have this need?" and "Who ultimately defines success for this learner?" can help point to a potential client for open workshops. Likewise, these questions may also point to a group of stakeholder individuals who become a client group. To illustrate this, let's look at two of the needs just listed that library staff targeted for an open workshop.

At the reference desk undergraduate students seem to be confused about finding books and journals in the catalog

In this scenario, undergraduate students are the targeted learners. Who is the client? Ask: *Why does the learner have this need?* What's the point? Are these users trying to get an A on their research paper? If so, who decides what is an A or not? If the majority of these students seem to be first-year English Composition students, a good bet is that the person who will judge the students' ultimate success in the workshop would be their English Composition instructor. The director of the English Composition program might be included as well if she is setting instructional standards to be met by all the English Composition courses. The client, then, might be a group of stakeholders that includes some English Composition instructors and the director of the program.

Job seekers continuously come in asking for help doing company research

Who is the client? Ask: *Who ultimately defines success for the job seeker?* In this case it's the person who is hiring the job seekers. That's your client. Of course, there are many people involved in hiring, so in this case you might pull together a client group that includes human resources staff from nearby companies, headhunters, and perhaps some managers or leaders in the key industries in your area. As I will discuss later, the more specific your client or client group, the more useful your workshop objectives will be to that client. In this case the client group may be narrowed by industry and by job level. The less specific you are in defining your client or client group, the more you risk creating a workshop that doesn't work very well for anyone in particular.

Workshop Participant as Client

In some cases, the workshop designers may not have answers to the preceding questions and may conclude that there is no client at all. The learners are also the clients when

> The learners will define their own success
>
> The learners know exactly what they need to know to be successful

Common examples of this include "Introduction to the Internet" workshops offered by the New York Public Library and many others. These workshops are designed for patrons who are recreational web users. There are no client stakeholder groups, no clients calling the library to ask that these be offered. No external person or group will decide if the learner is a successful recreational web user. The learners know that what they really need to be successful is to be able to connect to the Internet, do some basic searching, and use an e-mail account. The only people judging whether or not the workshop time was well spent are the learners themselves. So in this case the self-identified workshop participants are the clients.

A representative group of these learners can therefore stand in as a client group and be part of the needs assessment. This is important: just because there is no external client or client group doesn't mean that you're off the hook. You still have a client—the learner—and a needs assessment to conduct.

Adding a SME to the Mix

Apart from the client or client group, there may be another player to consider during the needs assessment. A SME (pronounced "smee") is a "subject matter expert." In the training field, instructional designers do not always have the expertise they need in the area they are designing for, and so they call in a SME to help with the content of the training. The SME makes sure the instructional designer identifies the important content to cover, understands the content reasonably well, and anticipates problems the learners may have with the content. The information the SME provides, coupled with the client assessment, helps ensure that the workshop teaches the right things in the right ways.

In the library world, we as librarians or library staff are usually our own SMEs. This is good news because it means less work for us, but it can be a problem if we are not working closely with a client: we run an even greater risk of designing our goals, objectives, and content in an information vacuum, disconnected from the greater goals of our client.

THE PROCESS FOR IDENTIFYING CLIENT NEEDS

If the library workshop design is not teaching what needs to be covered, and if the learners are not ultimately successful in the execution of their research or project, the workshop is not a success. In this case *need* is defined by an exploration of what it will take for the learner to be successful in the eyes of the client. What does the client want the learner to be able to do differently or better? How will the library workshop make a difference in the learners being successful *as defined by the client*? For example:

Does the community program director client need his staff to find better-quality grants?

Does the eighth-grade debate club advisor client need his students to be able to find facts and figures to support their arguments in the upcoming debate event?

Does the head of reference client need her staff to create and post web pages more quickly and efficiently?

Does the faculty client need her students to be more discerning consumers of information and choose higher-quality references?

The design process therefore begins with an assessment of the needs of the client for whom the workshop is being designed.

Methods for Identifying Client Needs

There are a number of ways to identify client needs:

- Analysis of previous learners' products (such as annotated bibliographies or research papers) and research logs
- Face-to-face interviews
- Focus groups
- Phone interviews
- E-mail interviews with follow-up
- Surveys

Let's take a look at each of these individually.

Analysis of Previous Learners' Products and Research Logs

Getting hold of previous learners' products or of research logs can produce a gold mine of information about what the learner needs help with. Writing samples, for example, can reveal gaps in the use of formats or in particular types of information. They may show an inability to critically evaluate sources or to build evidence for an effective argument. Web page designs may show the sophistication—or lack thereof—of use of web design techniques. If you are lucky and obtain research logs (or journals), these may show what errors, misconceptions, or difficulties the learners have. All of this information is invaluable in a needs assessment.

Interviews

Although it's tempting to conduct assessment interviews over the phone or by e-mail, in an ideal world the instructional designer would make a face-to-face appointment with the client. Holding a face-to-face interview indicates commitment to the workshops and gives the client a sense of importance. In this case flattery may, in fact, get you somewhere! The client begins to feel like a co-creator of the workshop. This instills a greater sense of ownership and buy-in and can pay off in many ways. More important, however, it gives the designer an opportunity to understand the issues and needs of the client.

Focus Groups

In cases where the client is actually a large group, the designer can hold a focus group or a series of focus groups. Focus groups can be made up of a subset of your client group (for example, a group of human resources specialists and headhunters). Try to find and invite the most important members of the group—the ones with the most power and influence within the larger client group. You want the larger group to be able to say things like, "Oh, I think Sandy and Phil worked on that workshop. They know what they're talking about and so this workshop must be pretty good. I better make sure my colleagues/staff/students go to this too." Most focus groups have four to eight participants in them and some incentive or reward for participation. Make a phone call to potential focus group participants and ask them what might entice their peers to come. Faculty or community members might expect a free lunch, students a monetary incentive or extra credit in a course, business leaders free membership in the Friends of the Library or a classy freebie. Regardless of incentives or rewards, try to spring for beverages and snacks. These can do wonders at helping to make the group feel more relaxed and comfortable.

Next, take some time to consider the pros and cons of getting a facilitator who is not connected to the project or even to the library itself. In my experience, having the instructional designer facilitate his or her own focus groups can be problematic. Focus group participants will sometimes defer to the expertise of the designer or ask the designer expert-like questions that put the designer in a difficult position as facilitator. It is also sometimes challenging for the designer to let go of an aspect of the topic they think is essential (e.g., "But of course conducting an advanced search is essential") even as they hear contradictory information from the participants. An "outside" facilitator does not carry any preconceived notions of what should or should not be covered and is not labeled an "expert." On the other hand, having been a fly on the wall at many of my focus groups, it can be frustrating not being able to jump into the discussion to ask crucial follow-up questions. These have to wait for follow-up phone calls or discussion at the end of the focus group.

One method to consider using in these focus groups is a brainstorming process. Begin by asking participants to identify everything they think is important about the topic from their perspective. Have an assistant capture these on the flipchart without discussion or evaluation. Next eliminate redundancies, group similar items, and discuss unclear items. Once the list is reorganized, use the bulk of the time to open up discussion about the items on the list. Finally, before dispersing, allot the participants a certain number of sticky dots, or check marks that they can make with markers, to indicate how important each item is for them in the workshop design. For those who like formulas, the general rule of thumb is to count up all the items and divide by six to get the number allocated to each participant. Instruct participants that they can put as many of their allotment on one item as they think is important. If there is still time, facilitate a discussion about this prioritization.

> **Tip**
>
> For help creating a script, administering, and analyzing focus groups, see Richard Krueger's classic book on the topic, *Focus Groups: A Practical Guide for Applied Research*, now in its third edition (Sage, 2000).

Surveys

There are several ways to use surveys in this step:

As a precursor to in-depth conversations

> Survey respondents can self-identify on the survey as being interested in being interviewed or being part of a focus group.

As a way to check that the larger client group is in agreement with the interviewees you already spoke with

> You might include questions that ask respondents to prioritize items that focus group participants identified, for example.

In lieu of interviews or focus groups

> Surveys can be used when you want to reach a large client group and do not have the time for interviews or focus groups, when anonymous information is important, when you want to report uniform data, or when you cannot get the attention of the clients for in-person interviews.

One of the main challenges with surveys is that they are very difficult to write without including our biases and mental models. Ideally, therefore, the survey should be carefully written after a series of interviews or focus groups in which the vocabulary, mental models, and ideas from these groups provide the basis for the survey design. If that is not feasible, at least include in the survey open-ended questions that will capture the participants' way of thinking and their exact wording and phrases, which will be useful later. At the least, perhaps you could add a request that those interested should call you and relay the information to you over the phone.

There are a number of free or low-cost net-based survey sites that you can use (e.g., Survey Monkey and Zoomerang). Receiving responses electronically will cut down considerably on the time it takes to analyze respondents' feedback.

Questions to Explore in a Needs Assessment

The following are some questions that may be helpful in designing a client interview.

What is it that your [colleagues/staff/students] need to be able to do?

Start with the big picture here—do not yet narrow down this answer to what exactly the workshop should cover. In many cases the client may not even know this. Remember, you are the library SME (subject matter expert), not them. Let the clients talk from their perspective as a faculty member grading papers, or as a community director trying to attract more grants, for example. They don't need at this point to talk about using a specific database or the pros and cons of teaching students to utilize thesaurus terminology. Spend the time trying to understand what the learner ultimately needs to do. This will help set your goals for the workshop and begin to flesh out potential marketing materials. As with all questions, be sure to capture the clients' exact wording and phrases for possible future use.

What would it look like to you (the client) if the learner did this exceptionally well?

This question begins to set the bar at the high end and helps you begin to assess the performance standards you will be aiming for and how you might evaluate them. It also gets the clients excited about the possibility of this workshop. If your clients are excited, they will deliver learners to your door. If not, you may end up either teaching reluctant, bored participants, or perhaps, if it is an "open" workshop—hardly any at all.

*Given all this, what are those things that you think absolutely
need to be taught in the workshop?*

Despite the fact that the clients are not the SME and you are, listen carefully to what they think should be covered. Are they adamant, for example, that a Google Scholar workshop should include a segment on where Google Scholar fits into an informed scholarly research approach? Do they feel that a segment on understanding the Dewey decimal system is crucial? Notice what they don't say. Hold onto these and at the very end of the conversation, ask them about these: "So, you didn't mention anything about advanced keyword searching. Do you feel that this is less important to your learners' success than these other things?" Ultimately, you are now beginning to identify possible content and a priority list for that content. Later in the design process, you will bring this information to bear with your own expertise to make decisions in this area. For the time being, however, just collect this information.

*What would it be helpful for me to know about the learners?
What kinds of approaches to teaching are they most accustomed to?*

Make sure you hear about the learners' current knowledge and skills in respect to the topic, their preexisting biases or opinions about the topic, and how the client thinks these learners learn best. What other characteristics of the learners might affect their success in the workshop or, ultimately, at their final task or product (such as their paper)?

All of this information will be extremely helpful in the next step of the design process, but by capturing it here, you eliminate having to come back again to your client for input.

*Why would you (the client) be willing to have the learners
attend this workshop?*

At this point your answers should start to look redundant, but it is often at the very end of the discussion that the client finally comes out with the perfect workshop goal or the perfect addition to the workshop content that you hadn't yet thought of. Again, capture as much of this as possible.

CODING WHAT YOU'VE LEARNED

Once the needs assessment is conducted and the client has gone, the designer will have a pile of audiotapes, pages of notes, or survey responses to comb through. In the best-case scenario the audiotapes and notes will be exact transcriptions, rather than interpretations by the facilitator, interviewer, or observers. The next challenge is to code these data into categories. Use exact words, phrasing, and sentences that come straight from the client's mouth as much as possible. Refrain from interpretation. The categories for coding can include the following:

Major drivers for the workshop

What difference will this workshop make for the learners? Why will this workshop be worth their time? This will map most directly to the first question above, "What is it that your colleagues/students/staff need to be able to do?" but as with all the categories, go through all the data to cull all the times major drivers were discussed.

Performance standards

What does it mean to the client that the learners have been successful? What does marginal success look like? This will map most directly to the second question above: "What would it look like to you if the learners did this exceptionally well?" You may also ascertain this if you are able to look at past learners' products or research logs that have been graded or marked by the client.

Content

What content does the client feel is important and what content superfluous for their definition of learner success? This will map most directly to the third question above, "Given all this, what are those things that you think absolutely need to be taught in the workshop?"

Learner analysis

What information about the learners do the client or the research logs or products relay? This category gives the designer a jump-start on the next step in the design process—the learner analysis. At this point just code all the data that would increase understanding of the learners. This will map most directly to the fourth question above, "What would it be helpful for me to know about the learners? How do you tend to teach them (if applicable)?" Or, "What kinds of approaches to teaching are they most accustomed to?"

Marketing material

What information will be helpful in subsequent marketing of the workshop? This will map most directly to the last question above, "Why would you be willing to have the learners attend this workshop?" The next section of this chapter addresses the role of the needs assessment in marketing.

USING THE NEEDS ASSESSMENT IN MARKETING

For those instructional designers who are responding to a request from a client for a specific workshop, marketing is a moot point. But for those instructional designers offering open workshops, no one wants to go through all this work for only a handful of workshop participants. For this group, the needs assessment does double duty. Not only does it provide critical information for the design of the workshop—it provides fabulous marketing material.

The needs assessment, in fact, becomes a marketing tool in and of itself. By involving the client from the beginning, your marketing efforts have already begun. Add to this the richness of information the needs assessment provides for marketing materials, and the time involved in needs assessment becomes well worth it.

Workshop Goals and Titles

An on-target workshop title and goal is a great marketing tool. The first thing you want to look for is a clearly articulated need that will be met by the workshop. Keep it from their perspective, using their words if possible. Examples include

- Find high-quality grants
- Find facts and figures to support arguments in your next school debate
- Create web pages more quickly and efficiently

This need can be translated directly into a title or subtitle for the workshop:

- Getting Grants: Finding High-Quality Grants at the Library
- Winning Debates: Find the Facts and Figures You Need to Win
- Quick and Efficient Web Page Design

Next capture the way that the client talks and thinks about these needs. Translate this into a workshop description.

Workshop Descriptions

A good title and workshop description can be just the incentive it takes to get clients committed to sending their colleagues/students/staff or to get a potential learner to attend the workshop. Here is the original description of a Dreamweaver workshop for library staff that was offered to me and my colleagues several years ago: "Work with Dreamweaver windows, menus, launcher, and palettes, page properties and text." I did not find this description to be particularly enticing, and in fact it made me question whether in fact I really needed to go at all. Would this kind of workshop help me on my job? What would I be able to do differently after learning this? Even if the content of this workshop was exactly what I needed, the goal of the workshop as stated in the description appeared to be a mismatch with my own goals. This was clearly an unsuccessful marketing message for me.

The marketing field has much to teach librarians about creating effective workshop descriptions. Robert Middleton is a marketing expert who works with independent professionals on designing effective marketing. He gives these professionals the following advice:

Build your case by explaining whom it's for

"This workshop was developed exclusively for library staff who create library web pages by hand coding or by WYSIWYG applications and who are now looking for a more robust authoring tool."

Build your case by explaining what will happen if they do it

"Library staff who attend this training will be able to reduce their turnaround time in getting content up on the Web and will have the tools to be more creative web page designers."

Build your case by showing how it works

"This Dreamweaver workshop works because we don't just show staff what to do; instead, we allow time for each participant to create an actual page using the tools they learn in the workshop."

Pull all these sentences together, for what would have been a much more effective workshop description:

This workshop was developed exclusively for library staff who create library web pages by hand coding or by WYSIWYG applications and who are now looking for a more robust authoring tool. Staff who attend this training will be able to reduce their turnaround time in getting content up on the Web and will have the tools to be more creative web page designers. This Dreamweaver workshop works because we don't just show staff what to do; instead, we allow time for each participant to create an actual page using the tools they learn in the workshop.

What a difference!

A rhetoric class at the University of Minnesota reinforced this notion that workshop names and descriptions can make or break a workshop. The class conducted a usability evaluation on the library's web page that lists open workshops and their descriptions and allows students to register. One of the problems the class identified was that the workshop descriptions were confusing. The usability test participants didn't know why they would need to take a given workshop. The rhetoric class pointed out that the descriptions were written from a librarian-centric position that didn't make sense to students. At the least, the workshop descriptions should not be a de-motivator for the client or learners, and at best they should be one of your best marketing techniques for the workshop.

Note that good workshop titles and descriptions are also useful when workshop participants are being "forced" to attend by a professor or supervisor or other authority. A compelling description has the possibility of creating some enthusiasm and interest in learning. It is always far easier to teach open, willing learners than those who are shut down and annoyed about being there.

COSTS OF SKIPPING STEP 1

Training and education are often substantial time and money investments, especially if travel is involved. When a participant leaves a workshop having learned little or nothing, there is a nonmonetary cost to the library. And when their faculty member or employer had required or highly encouraged the students or staff to complete the workshop and yet it still did not make a difference in their ultimate performance, then there may be a far bigger cost to the library. Although the client may come back and work with the library instructor again and communicate his or her needs and definition of success, if the instructor continues to ignore this information the client will inevitably move on.

It is possible that the now former client may decide that *all* library workshops are unsuccessful. This is how word spreads. Marketing professionals tell us that one dissatisfied customer tells many others about their experience. At the academic library level, we see this when we find that over time an entire department has stopped scheduling any instruction at all with their library liaison. Word got around. But then, when a new liaison is established with that department who is a more skilled instructor and marketer of services, slowly the instructional requests grow once again.

Before jumping in to create and deliver a workshop, make sure you conduct a needs assessment to ensure that the workshop will be valuable to a client and learners and that the content is completely on-target and an important contribution to the learners' ultimate success.

SUMMARY

Conducting a needs assessment is well worth the investment. It ensures that the designer is spending the instructor's and the learners' time wisely. It also helps the designer craft a workshop title, description, goals, and content areas to include or not include in the workshop. An effective title, description, and goals can go a long way in enticing clients to send their learners and in encouraging learners to show up and dive in.

The first step in a needs assessment is identifying the client (whether a person or group) with whom to conduct the needs assessment. The client may be someone who has directly commissioned the creation of the workshop, a person or group who are outside stakeholders in the success of the learners, or a representative group of the learners themselves. There are several ways to investigate their needs: using focus groups, conducting interviews and surveys, or analyzing an end product such as former papers that were written for a class or research logs from previous projects.

Case Study

This case study continues the story of the University of Minnesota's Unravel the Library workshop design process. As was mentioned, the design team identified the English Composition program as the client for the workshop, since the majority of first-year students write their first research paper in this program. Once the English Composition program was identified as the major client, the first order of business was to conduct the needs assessment.

To begin this process, the team interviewed one of its own members—the library liaison to the program—about the English Composition Department's curricular needs that she had identified over the course of her contact with the department. This was a great start. But in order to assess whether this information had changed or anything was missing and to enlist the support of the program, the design team created some tailored focus group questions for a key group of instructors and teaching assistants in the program. A free lunch was offered as incentive for participation, and a trained focus group facilitator from the library was enlisted to run the focus group. Seven instructors, the director of the program, and the assistant director all participated.

The focus group helped the design team come to a shared understanding that the overall need of the English Composition course in relation to the library is to enable students to find several books and articles on a particular topic. This was fairly obvious—the designers didn't need to conduct focus groups to discover this. But what was interesting to the design team was that the English Composition instructors not only stressed *scholarly* books and articles, but also insisted that one of the most useful things we could do for them was to teach their students how to figure out if their book or article was scholarly or not. They also did not want us to spend any time teaching Google or even Google Scholar, and in fact several participants vehemently protested at even the possibility that the library would cover that topic.

This information was worth its weight in gold. English Composition instructors frequently attest that the "scholarly vs. popular" section of the workshop is what makes the workshop so worth the time of their students. They also believe that because of their input, the library workshop focuses on the most important information that will help their students be successful. Because the instructors emphasize the value of these workshops to their students, the students required to attend the workshop know that what they learn will probably directly help them do well on their required research paper.

The design team therefore received a double benefit from conducting the focus groups: the identification of a highly useful workshop from the clients' perspective, and the facilitation of a high level of confidence in the workshops.

Are You All Set?

Have you

- ✔ Identified your client or client group?
- ✔ Conducted an assessment with your client or client group?
- ✔ Articulated the major need of your workshop based on your client or client group?
- ✔ Coded all the information you've collected?
- ✔ Identified which possible workshop content to include—and what not to include?
- ✔ Begun to identify a title and description as a component of marketing the workshop?

Analyze Learners

Often librarians must have enough flexibility to teach widely disparate learner groups. Depending on the type of library we work in, one day we might be teaching a class of senior citizens, the next day a sixth-grade history class, and the next staff from a particular department. These groups will have different learner characteristics and learner preferences. In teaching, one size does not fit all. Learners come with very different backgrounds, research experiences, mental models of the research process, skills, and abilities. For an instructional designer to grasp all of this without conducting a learner analysis would be nearly impossible.

A learner analysis is an opportunity to get inside the heads of the learners so that the designer or team can design a workshop that effectively reaches them. An important part of this is understanding how the learners think about the library and the research process. A learner analysis conducted at the University of Minnesota for a revision of the online tutorial showed just how different are the mental models of the research process between librarians and undergraduate students. These differences are probably not that much different from other learner groups.

> For students, research is a means to an end; for librarians, it is the end.
>
> For students, a good grade is valued; for librarians, good research is valued.
>
> For students, research is—or is expected to be—fast and easy; for librarians, research is complicated.
>
> For students, research is simply something you do; for librarians, it is something to learn to do.
>
> For students, learning is best done through games and interactivity; for librarians, through books and pathfinders.

Tip

To read more about this research, see an article I wrote with my colleague Karen Beavers called "Going Mental: Tackling Mental Models for the Online Library Tutorial at the University of Minnesota Libraries," published in *Research Strategies* 18, number 1 (2001).

The differences between just this one group (undergraduate students) and librarians illustrate the vast gulf that can exist between the way that we in libraries think and the way our users think. A popular quote in the usability field that is sometimes attributed to Dick Miller from Hewlett-Packard applies well to learner analysis: "Know thy user, for they are not you." Not only are learners quite different from librarians, they are not very much like each other either. The differences among learner audiences — between first-year and fourth-year undergraduates, between undergraduates and graduates, between students in different upper-level curriculums, between Baby Boomers, Generation Ys, Net Gens, and seniors, between social workers and business executives — call for careful consideration. In addition, the way each of these learners learns best gives us additional considerations during this phase of our research.

Although you might be offering a session attended by a mix of these learners, focus here on a target learner group that your client has helped you identify. Designing one workshop to meet the needs of a number of learner groups is difficult at best. It is better to redesign the workshop for another target group after completing your initial design process.

PROCESS FOR CONDUCTING A LEARNER ANALYSIS

At this point the instructional designer already has a head start on the learner analysis from client interviews, surveys, or focus groups conducted during the needs assessment (see previous chapter). Now it is time to delve further with actual learners or representatives from the learner group. A good learner analysis helps the designer to

- Design a workshop that starts with where the learners are
- Use teaching methods that are more conducive to their learning
- Pitch the workshop at the right level

Methods for Learner Analysis

The methods for conducting a learner analysis are similar to those used in the needs assessment:

- Face-to-face interviews
- Focus groups
- Phone interviews
- E-mail interviews with follow-up
- Surveys
- Analysis of previous learners' evaluations of similar workshops
- Surveys of the literature on characteristics of the target learners

Identifying Participants

Most of these methods cannot be done alone by the designer. Just as in the needs assessment, the designer will have to identify appropriate people to participate in this step. Questions to assist with this process include

Are the actual learners who would be in your workshop available?

> For example, if the workshop is being designed for a specific department's employees, can these employees be surveyed, interviewed, or scheduled for focus groups?

Are future, potential learners available?

> For example, if the workshop is being designed for graduate students in the History Department, are they already enrolled or registered and able to be contacted?

Are former learners available?

> For example, if the workshop is being designed to help debate students find facts and statistics that they need, are soon-to-graduate high school debate students available who could impart advice and insight that might help their junior debate teammates?

The main difference here is that the incentives for participation may need to be more compelling than those for the client. Creating an incentive that is effective enough to entice people to participate while not being excessive is a tricky balance. Ask a few potential participants for feedback about what might be adequate.

Areas to Explore

What are general characteristics of the target learners that may affect their learning?

Are the learners returning students who lack confidence and are intimidated by a modern library? Are they savvy web surfers? Do they understand the importance of using a library? Are they in an early development stage when they are still uncomfortable with ambiguity and complexity? Are they a group that has worked together a lot in the past and are comfortable together, or are they strangers to each other? Are they motivated to learn about your topic, or will they attend only because someone required it? What other learner characteristics might influence your workshop design?

What prerequisite knowledge, skills, and attitudes do the learners already have about the topic covered in the workshop?

What do they already know about libraries and research? What else do they know that is transferable? What attitudes, assumptions, and expectations will they have coming into your workshop?

What are these target learners' predominant learning styles?

Do they learn best by receiving a lot of content through lectures, by in-depth handouts, by an open laboratory approach, by interactivity, by games? What do they characterize as peak learning experiences? What approaches to teaching will work best for them, and what might turn them off to learning?

WHAT ARE LEARNING STYLES?

There are a number of different learning style models. Here I will use Peter Honey and Alan Mumford's learning styles categories developed from David Kolb's work. Honey and Mumford identify four predominant types of learners: activists, reflectors, theorists, and pragmatists (see figure 2-1).

Although any given classroom will have learners in each one of the quadrants shown in the figure, this step is your chance to see if the particular learning group you are working with tends to fall most often in one or two categories. Often certain disciplines and professions tend to focus on a certain quadrant, and this can draw in learners to that discipline who happen to be strong in that learning style. A graduate-level philosophy course, for example, may be filled with theorists. In contrast, an upper-level course in business management may be heavily weighed toward pragmatists.

Likewise, if the learners have been together as a learning cohort prior to coming to your workshop, they may be accustomed to being taught in a certain style. Spending an hour lecturing to a class full of learners accustomed to hands-on active learning may be less effective for that group than a hands-on active library workshop. On the other hand, asking students accustomed to listening and observing to actively learn with little lecture or demonstration might be an equally difficult adjustment to ask them to make.

If there are particular learning style preferences or habituated teaching styles that the learners are used to, this information will be important during steps 12 and 13 when the designer chooses appropriate teaching methods.

Note: A good analysis of Honey and Mumford's work is in Barbara Allan's *Training Skills for Library Staff* (Scarecrow, 2003).

FIGURE 2-1   Honey and Mumford's four predominant types of learners

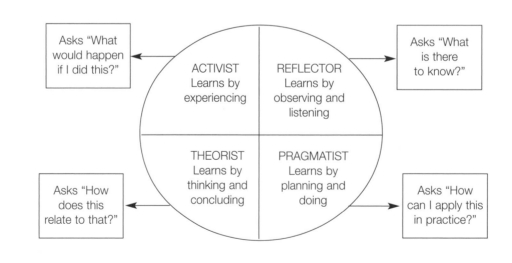

Questions to Ask

These are some possible questions to ask the learners:

What are the biggest challenges you face as a (student/employee/citizen, etc.)?

What do you think about libraries and library research?

Have you ever done any library research (if applicable to your workshop topic)? If so, what did you do? How did you do it? What did you think about your experiences?

What do you know already about _____[fill in with your workshop topic]_____?

If you had to go to a workshop on this topic, what would you like to learn?

Describe the best class or workshop you've ever taken and why you liked it so much.

Who is your favorite teacher and why?

Think of a time when you learned a lot. Why do you think you were able to learn so much?

Not all learning types are plucked from the same tree.

Advice for a Quick and Painless Learner Analysis

For many instructional designers, there may be neither enough time nor the desire to conduct comprehensive research on the target learners. Here are some quick ways to get some indication as to what your learners' characteristics and preferences are.

> Do a literature search. Many librarians have given talks and written papers about particular learner groups. See if you can find a match.
>
> If you have had the chance to work with these target learners in the past, try writing a profile of them. Try to answer the questions poised above on your own.
>
> Do you have any library colleagues who have worked extensively with the target learners? Take them out for coffee or call them and try to learn all you can from their experiences.
>
> Use information from the client gathered in the previous step's needs assessment. The client should have helped you narrow down the target learner group and better understand them.
>
> Look for clues in the evaluation sheets that people in your target group have filled out from other workshops.
>
> Ask the client to identify some people whom you can phone, e-mail, or better yet, meet in person. You might also ask the client where your target learners congregate and arrange to meet them there. Or you could try enticing them to meet you at your library. Food and freebie giveaways might work.

WHAT'S NEXT?

Once you've done your research on the target learners, take some time to write up your findings. Code the data into the three categories:

- Learner characteristics
- Previous knowledge, skills, and abilities
- Learning style preferences

Refer back to step 1 under the heading "Coding What You've Learned" and pull the appropriate information into this analysis.

If you're working alone, this data will serve as a future reminder, and if you're working in a group, this will allow you to make sure everyone is on the same page. Perhaps even more important, the next time a workshop is being designed for these target learners, the designer or team may be able to just pull out this profile and quickly move from step 1 to step 3. The learner analysis might also be written up in a report and shared with other library designers creating their own workshops for the target learners.

Regardless of how it might be used in the future, this write-up from the learner analysis, coupled with that from the needs assessment, forms the entire foundation for the rest of the instructional design process. Congratulations. Your hard work has netted you the information you need to build a highly effective, on-target workshop.

SUMMARY

The instructional designer can employ a number of methods to learn more about the learners, including interviews and focus groups, surveys, and analysis of previous learners' evaluations of similar workshops. These methods should help uncover various characteristics of the learners, including their learning style preferences and the knowledge, skills, and abilities they already have in regard to the topic. The data so collected is called a "learner analysis." A learner analysis contributes to a workshop design that is relevant, effective, and well suited to the target learners.

Case Study

The design team for the Unravel 2: The Research Process workshop had in the needs assessment stage already interviewed the English Composition liaison. This interview was very useful for the learner analysis. The liaison had shared what she knew of the mental models of research of first- and second-year students and what kinds of learning styles seemed to be most prevalent among them. The design team also reviewed the research by my colleague Karen Beavers and myself mentioned earlier, scanned the literature (the book *Educating the Net Generation* by Diana and James L. Oblinger [Educause, 2005] is extremely useful), and culled through information from the client meetings held during the needs assessment step.

Next the design team hosted a series of three focus group discussions with first- and second-year students so we could understand them even better. During the first design phase, students were recruited in the student union for a focus group immediately following the recruitment. Undergraduate students who said they had taken English Composition were then offered ten dollars for an hour of their time, plus cookies and beverages during the discussion. During a subsequent iteration of the Unravel the Research Process workshop several years later, students were recruited from a list of students who had previously taken the workshop. One focus group was offered directly after an Unravel workshop was given, and others were scheduled during unrelated times, within one to three months after the students had completed the workshop. All of these approaches garnered invaluable information about these learners.

The focus groups were moderated by a library staff member not involved in the design. The questions asked were similar to the ones suggested earlier in this chapter, and the answers were integrated with the data obtained from other areas of learner analysis. This created a very rich profile of the target learner group for the Unravel workshops. At this point the team set the learner profile aside to move on to the next step in the design process. Note that the information gathered was absolutely critical for those librarians on the design team who did not regularly work with the target learners and did not have a close understanding of them.

For those wanting a future glimpse into the impact the learner analysis had, here is a short preview. What this profile translated into is a very hands-on, quickly paced, and highly interactive workshop design where *all* learners participate. There is very little theory and lecture. Students learn and apply skills constantly throughout the workshop. And because of what we learned about their mind-sets and assumptions, the workshops are designed to convince students that the university libraries are a valuable, scholarly alternative to Google and that there are many tools and services designed to make their research process better, more efficient, and even painless.

Are You All Set?

Have you

✔ Identified ways to learn more about your learners?

✔ Conducted a learner analysis and come to better understand your learners?

✔ Captured the information you learned?

STEP 3

Brainstorm Content

Now that the designer better knows the needs of the client that the workshop will address (from step 1) as well as the prerequisite knowledge, skills, and attitudes of the learners (from step 2), the next step is to identify relevant workshop content. The good news is that brainstorming workshop content is one of the easiest steps in the entire design cycle. During this stage you have an opportunity to capture everything that you, the client, and the learners might want to have included in the workshop.

As you can imagine, there is usually no shortage of tips, instructions, or details that learners would need to know to be successful researchers. Just imagine pulling five librarians into a room and asking them to identify all the things they would want to teach their learners in a particular workshop. Do you think they'd come up with a fairly consistent list? Probably not. What one person thinks is good to know about can often make another look at that person flabbergasted. In the collaborative designs I have facilitated, at some point every single member of the group ends up incredulous, saying things like, "You teach *that* to (first-year students/faculty/graduates)?!" Regardless, the response is always to "put it on the list." All of these disparate ideas of what is important teaching content are encouraged.

PROCESS FOR A SUCCESSFUL BRAINSTORMING SESSION

This step in the design process can be completed in one or two brainstorming sessions. To prepare for it, the designer pulls together the right people to assist, reviews the relevant information from steps 1 and 2, and then is either prepared to do a lot of flipchart writing or requests an outside person to take notes during the session.

Form a Brainstorming Group

Partner and Team Designers

This is the ideal situation for a brainstorm, since it includes other individuals who have different ideas of what might be covered in the workshop. Set up a meeting time with your design partner or team in a space where you can write and post flipcharts on the walls for everyone to see. Decide if you need to (and can) find someone else to do the flipcharting for you.

Individual Designers

Individual brainstorming is limited to the creative boundaries of one person. This is not an ideal situation, but if it is necessary, the designer should set aside some quiet time away from their everyday work in a place or situation that might help them think creatively. Better yet, is there a colleague or two who teaches a similar learner or has a similar client, or who at least teaches similar content? In small libraries this may mean colleagues in nearby libraries, or colleagues from similar libraries who can get together on a conference call. If this is your situation, try setting up a speakerphone so you are free to type or write during the session.

Offer Some Background Review

Prior to the brainstorming session, ask the brainstorm participants to review the needs assessment and learner analysis data conducted in steps 1 and 2. More specifically, take time to identify the knowledge, skills, and abilities the learners may have that can act as a starting point when beginning the workshop. Ask the group to pay particular attention to the client's goals and definition of success. Also ask them to reflect on their experiences working in the past with this client (or type of client) and learners. What content did they think it was important to cover in those situations?

Ask the participants to review any other data that might help the group identify workshop content. Focus groups from other projects, usability tests from a website redesign, and workshop content or lesson plans from other workshops might all be instructive.

Although the background review can be done at the beginning of the meeting, it may be counterproductive to do it if the ensuing discussion leads to debate, conflict, criticism, and divergent opinions. This dynamic will make it difficult—if not impossible—to create an open, trusting, and relaxed brainstorming session. Instead, either hold the background review as a separate meeting in which you can have discussion and debate, or ask group members to individually browse through their materials ahead of time.

Conduct the Brainstorming Session

If the group does not already feel comfortable with each other, you or the facilitator (if you have one) may have to work extra hard to set a meeting tone that is conducive to brainstorming. For some people there will be a sense of risk involved in this process of putting their ideas and even their teaching practice out there for everyone to judge and criticize. Therefore, set the ground rules for brainstorming before beginning:

Remind the group that no idea is too preposterous and that one person's wild idea might be the catalyst for someone else's brilliant one.

Be clear that there will be no evaluation or critique during the brainstorming session. This will come later. Each person's role at this point is just to offer an idea and clarify it only to the point that everyone in the room understands it.

Review the process for the brainstorming session (explained next).

Once the ground rules are out of the way, give everyone ample time to individually brainstorm a list of all the possible content possibilities that might meet the client's needs. Ask them to do this in silence so that everyone has some time to think a bit and write down each idea they can think of. When the writing seems to have slowed, ask participants to come up with just one or two more ideas. It is often during this time in the process that people have their most productive thoughts.

If you are working in a group, use a flipchart and draw a margin near the left-hand side of the page. Then go around in a circle, with each person identifying only one item on their list at a time. Have someone capture the ideas on the flipcharts. Continue going around the circle several times, with everyone just mentioning one item at a time. When individuals are out of new ideas, they can pass until all ideas are exhausted. This process is called the nominal group technique. You should now have several flipcharts full of ideas.

These brainstorm items might range from the very broad, such as "How to evaluate information," to the very specific, such as "Use interlibrary loan for articles you can't find in the catalog." At this point just capture everything on a flipchart, no matter how broad or specific. As in all brainstorming, there is no right or wrong and there is no judging or supporting. Note that the more broadly you have defined the session given your discussion in steps 1 and 2, the longer and more unwieldy your brainstormed list of content ideas will be. This is why it is important to clearly identify your client and your learners' specific needs before you start the brainstorming process.

A word of caution about human dynamics during this process. Group brainstorming is one of those times when we reveal what we think is important to teach and we omit other things that our colleagues might believe are vehemently important. This can lead to moments of self-doubt for some, and outright scorn for others. A brainstorming meeting can therefore be one of the more important meetings to carefully facilitate. This is one of those times when you might consider bringing in an outside facilitator to ensure that the process feels safe and open.

Once all ideas are put out on the flipchart, individuals can ask for clarification. It is important that individuals use this time to fully understand what someone meant by their brainstormed idea, rather than critique it. Once everyone is satisfied that they understand what all items mean, the brainstorming step is complete.

SUMMARY

This step moves the designer from a focus on gathering background information to the identification of possible workshop content. The goal of the brainstorming session is to pull all the background information together that relates to content and then to round out that information with the librarians' own ideas. By using a brainstorming technique called the nominal group technique, the instructional designer can create a comprehensive, detailed list of possible workshop content.

Case Study

To prepare for the brainstorming session for Unravel the Library 2: The Research Process, the design team reviewed their notes from the needs assessment and learner analysis, as well as web usability results from a recent home page design. These usability results from a library website redesign were actually quite helpful. For example, the results showed that identifying an appropriate article index was not an intuitive or simple task. Prior to these tests, most of us as instructors tended to gloss over this step ("Click, here, click there, now you're in an article index!" they would demonstrate, and then move on to the actual searching). Given this new information that actually countered our previous knowledge about what parts of the research process were intuitive, the design team was sure to place "How to find and pick an article index from the library's web page" on the brainstorm list.

The following is an abbreviated list of brainstormed items from the University of Minnesota's Unravel 2: The Research Process workshop. This contains enough content for what could be several weeks of library instruction.

ABBREVIATED BRAINSTORM LIST FOR UNRAVEL 2 CONTENT
- What an article index is
- When to use an article index
- What a catalog is
- When to use a catalog
- Distinguishing indexes vs. web search engines
- WorldCat
- What we pay for—what we don't
- How to find and pick an article index from home page
- What if you don't get "full text"
- Boolean (AND/OR/NOT) searching
- Subject searching—controlled vocabulary
- Keyword—"uncontrolled" vocabulary

Natural language problems (e.g., typing "What is my opinion?" in Google)

Truncation

Limiting by date

Limiting by format

Searching by author and title keywords

Using advanced search screen in catalog

Finding e-journals through the catalog

Finding e-journals from e-journals list

Using e-journals

Output options (e-mailing citation) and full text

Can't find articles in catalog

Finding if library owns journals—interpreting holding records

Distinguishing between book and article citations

Getting the correct citation information in order to find a book or journal on the shelf

Where to go for help

How to know if something is popular or scholarly

Abbreviations for journal titles

Why everything isn't full text

Narrowing and defining topic (using subheadings in Expanded Academic Index)

Field searching (author, title)

All indexes are different (who publishes them?)

This brainstorm list overwhelmed the group with content ideas. No one person could have thought up all these topics. The next challenge was to filter through the list and choose the most critical items.

Are You All Set?

Have you

- ✔ Lined up your design partner, team, or willing colleagues to participate in a brainstorming session?
- ✔ Reviewed the information from steps 1 and 2?
- ✔ Reviewed any other information that might be useful, such as relevant usability test results that reveal access problems?
- ✔ Created a meeting tone that is conducive to brainstorming?
- ✔ Exhausted all possibilities and ideas from your brainstorm group?
- ✔ Sought clarification on the unclear items but refrained from critique?

Filter Content

You should now be facing a long, unwieldy list of possible content for your workshop. The next step is to eliminate the nonessential items and whittle down the list to something that can work in the allotted workshop time. But first, before doing this, make sure that everyone involved in designing the workshop understands the costs of loading on too much content.

BEWARE OF COGNITIVE OVERLOAD!

Fundamental to this step is a basic understanding of the perils of cognitive overload. Cognitive overload happens when the instructor's content exceeds the capacity of the student's working memory. According to writer and trainer Ruth Colvin Clark,

The brain's ability to process incoming information can slow nearly to a halt. This is why it is difficult to multiply 8,697 times 978 in your head without using an estimating technique. It becomes impossible simultaneously to hold the intermediate products of the multiplication in memory and continue processing the next numbers. When working memory has to hold even a small memory load, its ability to process new information degrades rapidly. This interferes with learning, which requires the processing of information. Thus, if you expect participants to learn, you cannot expect them also to hold information in working memory. (Ruth C. Clark and David Taylor, "The Causes and Cure of Worker Overload," *Training* 31, no. 7 [1994]: 40)

There is a wide gap between the working memory of a novice researcher and that of an expert. The learner analysis completed earlier in the design process is important groundwork for this step. How close is the learner to being a novice? The closer the learner is to being a novice, the faster he or she will experience cognitive overload.

In other words, the temptation to pack content into a workshop can hinder learning, especially since there is often only a limited time with our learners. And the negative consequences don't stop there. Clark explains that learners experiencing cognitive overload often believe that the problems they are having in the workshop are due to their own inadequacies as learners. They become frustrated and demoralized, lose their place, and fall behind. What is further disturbing is that often these learners hide their failings so that you as a teacher may not even know that you have reached their learning limit.

> *Students aren't going to learn everything we have to teach them. It's better to focus on having them learn at least something. I've seen instructors who haven't gone through the instructional design process who spend so much time on things that are not important to the student's ability to learn what we want them to do. They spend minutes and minutes on it and then the students hit overload, and when it comes to the important stuff they're gone. It's important that we know that students aren't computers. They're not going to retain it all. You have to choose.*
>
> —Lynne Beck, Library Assistant, Government Publications Library, University of Minnesota Libraries–Twin Cities

LESS IS MORE

Continuous talking and demonstration of everything the student possibly might need to know lead to overload. Overload impedes learning. One of the goals of the workshop design, therefore, is to greatly reduce cognitive overload. In order to do this the design team needs to follow a "less is more" strategy. "Less is more" in practice means that the list of items that the designers think students vitally need to know must be very, very lean.

PROCESS FOR FILTERING CONTENT

The instructional design team begins by combing through every item on the brainstorm list and asking if the item is essential—if it is a "need-to-know" item—in order for the students to be successful in their course. Anything less than essential gets put on the "nice-to-know" list and is filed away for a future workshop design.

The inverted triangle shown on page 46 can help the design team make distinctions between the brainstormed items.

> *When I first began work as a teaching assistant for the library, I could not believe how emotional our design team members would get about need-to-knows and nice-to-knows. After teaching workshops for two years, I now understand the emotional part of the design process. There is so much information out there from which our students could benefit. Deciding what to teach them is tough, and it's easy to get your ego involved as you fight for what you believe is necessary. The struggle is worth it, though. In the end, we come up with a very impactful, fine-tuned workshop full of the essentials to get our students going in their research.*
>
> —Debra Payne Chaparro, PhD Student and Teaching Assistant, University of Minnesota Libraries–Twin Cities

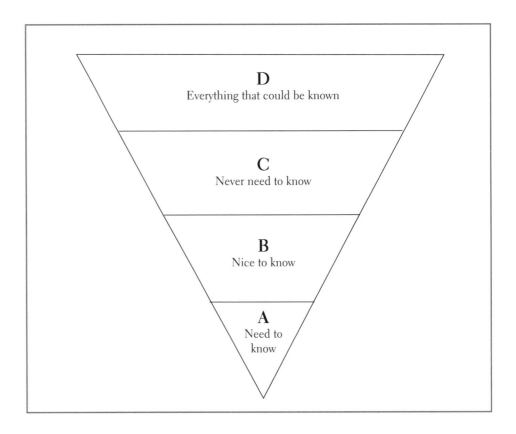

Information from the needs assessment and the learner analysis helps direct which items go where on this triangle. One target learner group's nice-to-know item may be another's need-to-know, and likewise, one's *never*-need-to-know may in fact be another's need-to-know. There are no hard-and-fast rules.

Because these decisions are difficult, the filtering process can represent the most contentious part of the team-based design process. If each member of the design team created the need-to-know list independently, there would be six or seven very different lists. If three or four design teams were designing the same workshop for different learners and clients, there might be even more variations. As a consequence, a disproportionate amount of time in the team-based instructional design process can be spent coming to consensus on this list.

Questions to Help Filter Items

Some questions that may help the design team filter items on the inverted triangle include:

Is this item critical for learner success? In other words, if the learners did not learn how to do this, would they still be able to do well enough to be deemed successful (by the client) in their paper/speech/project/etc.?

Can the learners (or will the learners) learn this content elsewhere?

Even if this item is important, is it important for these particular learners with this particular client?

Is it even possible to include this item in the time allotted for this workshop? Even if it can be squeezed in, would it just contribute to cognitive overload and damage the potential learning of other items on the need-to-know list?

The Finalized List

For team designers it may take more than one meeting to come to an agreement on the need-to-know list. In particularly difficult cases, some items may be kept on a "border" need-to-know with agreement that if it gets in the way of the learner learning the rest of the content, it would be downgraded to the "nice-to-know" list or moved off to a handout.

SUMMARY

One of the most important responsibilities of the instructional designer is managing cognitive overload. The mismanagement of cognitive overload can break a workshop. Every item in the brainstormed list must be rigorously critiqued and sorted into two categories: the essential need-to-know items and the nonessential items. Filtering content like this can be for many designers one of the most challenging steps in the entire design cycle.

Case Study

The initial brainstorm list for the Unravel 2 workshop design had more than thirty items on it. The filtering process was extremely difficult. We brought out the needs assessment and the learner analysis feedback again to help us prioritize items. We had long discussions about the merits of teaching each item and kept asking questions of each other like those listed earlier in the section "Questions to Help Filter Items."

After these discussions the design team reduced the brainstormed list down to nine items. This became the first filtered list and included:

What an article index is

When to use an article index

How to find and pick an article index from Research QuickStart [an online list of key indexes by topic—see http://research.lib.umn.edu/]

How to distinguish between popular and scholarly materials

The differences between keyword and subject searching

Finding good subject headings from a keyword search

Searching the catalog to find if the library owns a journal/book/newspaper

Where to go for help

Despite all the filtering we had done, the design team felt that this was probably still too many items for the need-to-know list. We decided to revisit the list further into the design process and held on to some hope that we might actually be able to keep all the items without overloading our learners. (You'll see further into the design process that we finally accepted that we were indeed putting our learners into overload with all these items, and so we had to make even more filtering decisions.)

Revisiting the learner analysis at this step was helpful because we had been focusing so much on client and curricular needs. The team realized that we had neglected to take into account any of the learners' content interests that might be different from the faculty or curricular interests. Although these content interests are not critical to the students' success in their English Composition course, the design team decided it was important enough to send satisfied students back to their faculty members with the sentiment that the workshop was worth it. Because of this we indulged ourselves with just one more item:

Identifying full text within article indexes

Although this is not an essential content item for being successful with the English Composition research paper, it is clearly something that students are eager to learn. But the real linchpin was the argument that for some students getting the full text online *is* an essential item for their success. With that argument won, it was included on the need-to-know list.

Are You All Set?

Have you

✔ Identified the essential "need-to-know" items on your brainstorm list?

Group Content

This next step helps make sense of the need-to-know list by grouping items into modules (or "chunks"). A one-hour workshop session may include two, three, four, or even five modules, each covering a discrete task or topic. In a grant research workshop, for example, there may be a module on "Identifying Community Grants," another on "Identifying State Government Grants," and perhaps a few other modules, depending on the scope of the workshop.

Grouping a workshop's content into modules serves several purposes:

Each module becomes a discrete unit of the final workshop.

The remainder of the design process can be done from start to finish one module at a time which ultimately expedites the process.

As a time-saver, designers might choose the option of only designing fully one module of the workshop and teaching the rest of it using their traditional design methods.

A particular module may be prioritized and subsequent modules may be put on the back burner.

Library instructors can use a module or two from one workshop and insert these into another workshop with a different, but similar, set of goals.

Each module has defined objectives, teaching methods, and fully developed teaching materials. This makes working with future clients easier because the librarian can provide a suite of clearly articulated teaching units from which clients can "mix and match" in a manner that best meets their needs.

Well-defined objectives, teaching methods, and teaching materials may also make it easier to go back to the current client to argue for more time for the workshop or for additional workshops in order to fit in another module or two or three that contain important content.

PROCESS FOR GROUPING

1. Group your brainstormed "need-to-knows" in outline form.

   There likely will be very broad items on your lists (such as "find an article") along with very specific ones that fall beneath these items (such as "Click on the full-text link to get to the article").

2. Look for gaps in your content.

   For example, you may have included "Click on the full-text link to get to the article," but not have any content on interpreting the SFX menu. Upon discussion this item may then become a new need-to-know and be included in the module. Be cautious, however, of too much "need-to-know creep" swelling the filtered list.

3. Order the modules.

   Arrange the modules roughly in chronological order from the beginning of the workshop through to the end. This will help you build transitions between modules later in the design process.

4. Design each module so that it can stand on its own.

   Because these modules might later be pulled from this particular workshop and added to others, it is wise to design a module in which a learner will be able to accomplish something useful *whether or not* they have been taught any of the other workshop content.

5. Be willing to revisit the module groupings further into the process.

   It is difficult at this stage to define accurately how large a particular module should be. Initially you may fit a large number of your filtered content items into one module, but later in the design process you may realize that you have too much and need to cut the module back down, divide the content into two separate modules—or even eliminate that module altogether.

6. Check that the modules still support the needs assessment and learner analysis feedback.

   This is another opportunity to make sure the design is not slipping away from the client's original needs.

SUMMARY

The need-to-know list should be organized into discrete modules that can be designed from start to finish one module at a time. Arrange the modules in outline form and order them roughly chronologically from the beginning of the workshop to its end. Although you will want to avoid "need-to-know creep," this is a good time to look for anything you might have missed in the list that would be essential to cover as a particular module.

The Unravel 2 design team was able to group the need-to-know items into five content area modules that reflected tasks the students needed to complete. The team arranged these tasks to reflect the sequential process a student might take when conducting his or her own research:

Finding Articles: Choosing an Article Index

What an article index is

When to use an article index

How to find and pick an article index from Research QuickStart (an online list of specific resources listed by subject)

Finding Articles: Searching for Articles

The differences between keyword and subject searching

Finding good subject headings from a keyword search

Catalog Searching for Known Items

Distinguishing between book and article citations

Searching the catalog to find if the library owns a journal/book/newspaper

Catalog Searching for Unknown Items

The differences between keyword and subject searching

Finding good subject headings from a keyword search

Distinguishing between Scholarly and Popular Sources

How to distinguish between popular and scholarly materials

As mentioned in the previous chapter, at first pass this list felt like a highly filtered effort. We had started with so much, and with so many ideas, and we had finally gotten down to what seemed most essential. Despite this, the modules had to be revisited and revised during subsequent steps of the design cycle. First, it became painfully apparent that a 60-minute session would be inadequate to effectively teach this amount of content, so the workshop time was extended to 75 minutes. But then, after piloting the workshop, we realized that even 75 minutes was not adequate and the team subsequently had to drop the "Catalog Searching for Unknown Items" module from the workshop—a painful decision for many of us. Although this module reinforced objectives from the "Finding Articles" module, it had redundancies we felt we could afford to forgo in hopes that "Finding Articles" would provide transferable skills to the catalog.

The final workshop design has only four content modules for a full 75 minutes of workshop time. Ideally we would have been able to fit in more modules, but the cost to the actual learning was too high. So in exchange for cutting out a bit of content, our learners are able to demonstrate to us that they have at least learned the content we kept. Not a bad trade.

Are You All Set?

Have you

✔ Grouped your list of need-to-know items into modules?

✔ Identified any missing gaps?

✔ Been rigorous in keeping a strict need-to-know list and kept those nice-to-know items from creeping in?

✔ Placed the modules in an order that would make sense for the learners?

✔ Double-checked that the needs assessment fits the modules and content chosen so far?

Create Task Analysis

During the brainstorming, filtering, and grouping steps, items tend to remain at a fairly high interpretive level. For example, think about the item "Choose an appropriate article index," which might appear on a brainstormed list. Ask several librarians what concrete steps they would advise the learner to take to accomplish this task and you will probably get several different responses. One librarian would advise the learner go to an article indexes page on the Web. Another would advise the learner to go to a pathfinder page. Another might devise a complex ten-step approach, while another would argue for an oversimplified three-step approach. Now is your chance to put all of these opinions, best practices, and approaches on the table for discussion and decision-making. Creating what is called a "task analysis" will help you do this.

A task analysis is a rigorous exercise that brings what is often an unconscious process to the conscious level. The task analysis breaks down a task into subtasks which are then broken down into specific steps.

WHY CREATE A TASK ANALYSIS?

By breaking down a task into subtasks and steps, the designer is forced to be very explicit in what the learners will be taught and in what the learners will be able to do after the workshop. This allows the designer to

- Identify the direct deliverables for the workshop
- Create clear and detailed handouts

- Clarify exactly what to test for during and at the end of the workshop
- Ensure that all learners are learning the same process if the workshop is given by multiple instructors or over a long period of time
- Make informed changes to the workshop if evaluations uncover problems with specific parts of the workshop
- Create an assessment tool that exactly mirrors the task analysis

CREATING A TASK ANALYSIS

There are different ways to create a task analysis. It can be put in a flowchart like the following task analysis chart, which shows one task and its components.

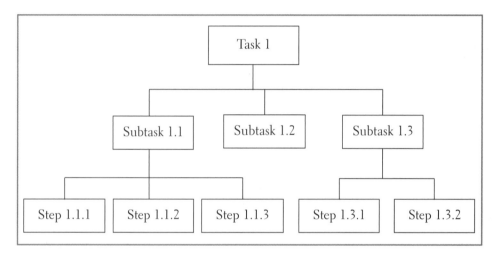

Alternatively, a task analysis can be created in a table format that shows more than one task, as in figure 6-1.

WRITING GUIDELINES

Tasks, subtasks, and steps describe what a person does. To write these:

- Start with an action verb
- Use a noun after the verb
- Keep it brief—avoid detail
- Avoid overlap between tasks

Tasks, subtasks, and steps *do not* include statements about:

- Attitudes (e.g., "Be cheerful when dealing with patrons")
- Goals or standards (e.g., "Maintain a high level of customer service")
- Knowledge (e.g., "Understand the food and drink policy")

FIGURE 6-1 Task analysis

Task	Subtask	Step
1. The first task. This represents a complete activity.	1.1. The first subtask breaks down the task into a manageable segment.	1.1.1. The steps involved in this subtask should be detailed enough so that the learner could follow without assistance. 1.1.2. Subsequent steps go here. 1.1.3. Etcetera.
	1.2. If there is a second subtask, it goes here.	1.2.1. This would be the first step for the second subtask. 1.2.2. Next step, etc.
	1.3. If there is a third subtask (or more) they continue to be listed here.	1.3.1. First step for the subtask 1.3 goes here. 1.3.2. Next step, etc.
2. The second task.	2.1. First subtask of second task.	2.1.1. First step for subtask. 2.1.2. Next step, etc.
	2.2. Second subtask of second task.	2.2.1. First step for subtask. 2.2.2. Next step, etc.

- Selection criteria or prerequisites (e.g., "Staff will have taken an introduction to the customer service workshop through Human Resources")

Common Action Verbs

Bloom's Cognitive Taxonomy provides a comprehensive list of action verbs that may be useful in formulating good statements:

A   activate, administer, acquire, approve, analyze, arrange, assist, assign, accept, adhere, anticipate, apply, adopt, advise

B   brief

C   conduct, confer, consolidate, consult, correlate, change, control, create, coordinate, coach, compile, cooperate, contract, contribute, communicate, classify, choose, calculate, collaborate, collect, check, compute, catalog, construct, count

D   develop, determine, direct, disburse, design, describe, demonstrate, discriminate, defend, decide, devise, discuss, disseminate, draft

E   ensure, evaluate, establish, execute, express, estimate, endorse, examine, experiment, exchange, explain, edit

F   formulate, forecast, facilitate, file

G   give, guide, generate, gather

H   handle, hold

I   interpret, issue, implement, identify, interview, instruct, inspect, initiate, inform, investigate, improve, inventory

J   justify

K   keep

L   layout, lecture, list

M   meet, maintain, measure, motivate, manipulate, manage, make, monitor, modify

N   negotiate

O   organize, operate, orient, obtain, observe, originate

P   proceed, prepare, perform, provide, process, plan, produce, promote, propose, publicize, program, practice, prove, participate, place, procure, prescribe, proofread

Q   question, query

R   review, research, revise, recommend, remove, request, reject, report, represent, relate, recognize, recount, reinforce, resolve, regulate, receive

S   supply, select, service, screen, serve, set, solve, state, secure, specify, stimulate, submit, supervise, score, search, study, survey, send, staff, suggest

T   train, transfer, test, tell, transcribe, translate, transmit, tutor, teach

U   utilize

V   volunteer, verify, validate

W   write

Many of you have seen Bloom's taxonomy or versions of Bloom's work all over the Internet. The original source for these is Benjamin Bloom's 1956 book *Taxonomy of Educational Objectives: The Classification of Education Goals: Handbook I, Cognitive Domain* (Longmans, Green).

Try It Out

You are helping a colleague create a workshop on basic HTML. The learners are new support staff who are high school gradu-

> *I think we need to be careful not to oversimplify our content. If we don't offer challenging content, students will tune us out. You don't go to a doctor to learn about Tylenol. Let's not dumb down library information either.*
>
> —Susan Gangl, Reference Librarian and Graphic Designer, University of Minnesota Libraries–Twin Cities

ates. You cannot assume that they have any previous experience or training with computers. Given this background, check the items on the following list that are actually tasks:

_____ Click on File and then Save As

_____ Tags are surrounded by the less than (<) and greater than (>) symbols

_____ Type in the name of your file: a:/xxxx.html

_____ Review the page using Internet Explorer

_____ Create a basic web page

_____ Cascading style sheets are not required

_____ Save and name the file

To see how you did, turn to page 60 for the answers.

PROCESS FOR ANALYZING TASKS

Breaking tasks down into subtasks and steps can be a fairly untidy, nonlinear process. It is common to move from the task level to the step level and then find you have to move back up again to make the subtask and task either broader or narrower. Remember, the step level should be able to be completed by the learner without assistance. If you get down to the step level only to find that the step cannot be done by the user without assistance, that item is actually a subtask.

The following is a process for determining what are tasks, subtasks, and steps.

1. Start by identifying the tasks.

   An easy way to do this is to look back at the module groupings and the need-to-know items under each module that were created in the last chapter. Often these can be directly translated into the language of a task and/or subtasks. Sometimes a module may consist of two or three tasks, and other times a module may consist of just one task.

2. Determine the appropriate way to complete a task.

   This will depend on the learner group. As library experts we see the complexity, the contingencies, and the necessary alternatives to tasks. Our job is to understand the learners' developmental level. Younger students and new learners are not ready for complexity, contingencies, or alternatives. Their task analysis needs to be clear and unambiguous. Advanced learners, on the other hand, who have experience and prior knowledge of the task, can better deal with ambiguity. Their task analysis might include alternative routes and contingency plans. Know the learners, and design the level of simplicity or complexity of the task for those particular learners.

3. Identify what the learners already know.

   What the learners already know helps to determine at what level of detail a step should be written. If you are training senior citizens how to use the

Web, for example, and they have never used a computer before, you might have to include a step that specifies to the learners that they have to move the cursor across the screen and another step specifying the action of left-clicking on the mouse. For another learner group, you would never think to break down a procedure into such minutiae because you know your learners already have these skills. Their task analysis will look very different from the beginners' group. A task analysis, therefore, may be done at many levels—novice, intermediate, advanced, expert. It is important to match the task analysis to the level of the learners. This is, accordingly, another good time to revisit needs assessment and learner analysis feedback that might help with understanding the prior knowledge of the learners and what their current skill level with the material might be.

4. Check your assumptions.

Even though you may have decent needs assessment and learning analysis data, beware of your hidden assumptions. For each step in the task analysis, ask if there are any inaccurate assumptions of the learners' prior knowledge. You may have to go back to the client or some representative learners to check these assumptions. Do the learners really know how to use a mouse? Do they know how to save or open a file? Do they know how to choose from a list of subject pathfinders the one that relates most appropriately to their research topic? If only a minority of the learners don't know how to do something (such as operate a mouse), make that prerequisite knowledge for the workshop if possible. You may even have a way for students to take a tutorial, another workshop, or a quiz to illustrate that they have the prerequisite knowledge.

5. Review the need-to-know list again.

Are each of the subtasks essential? Are each of the steps essential? Is there anything here that can move to the nice-to-know list? Set aside the nice-to-know items for possible inclusion in a handout or future workshop.

Issues and Conflicts

If more than one person is working on the workshop design, the task analysis process is bound to surface contrasting processes and various best practices. It may even reveal major differences in understanding the need-to-know item that the task falls under. The design team may have thought they were all on the same page, but this is where the design team *really* finds out if that's the case.

Even though this may be difficult, keep challenging each other in the team until finally everyone has come to some level of consensus that the best process for the task and learners was identified.

This task analysis will later be the way the library instructor teaches how to complete the task and serves as the basis of an instructional handout on the task.

SUMMARY

Creating a task analysis challenges the designer to identify appropriate level steps, subtasks, and tasks for a particular group of target learners. The final product is a detailed map of what the learners will be able to do and how they will go about doing it. This will help clarify to others (clients, other library staff, etc.) exactly what the learners will be able to do after the workshop and for whom the content is appropriate. Future steps will benefit from the development of the task analysis.

Case Study

Normally the process of teaching students how to distinguish whether a source is popular or scholarly varies according to the instructor. Analyzing this task helped the Unravel the Research Process design team come to a shared agreement of what they thought were the most important components of the process. Figure 6-2 shows the main way the design team conceptualized this process.

This task analysis forced the group to take a fairly complex task and design it to work at the first-year undergraduate level. There was abundant discussion about this level of simplicity. The group, for example, questioned whether or not it should bring "gray literature" (i.e., literature that combines scholarly and popular characteristics) into the task list. In the end, it was decided that gray literature should be a teaching point (see next chapter) that would only be included to encourage students to talk to their professors if the source they were using did not fall neatly into either the popular or the scholarly category.

FIGURE 6-2 Scholarly vs. popular task analysis

Task	Subtask	Step
1. Identify if my citation is scholarly or popular.	1.1. Identify if scholarly.	1.1.1. Check if the title of article uses specialized language of the discipline. 1.1.2. Check if the journal title is not something you'd see on the newsstand. 1.1.3. Check if the article is lengthy (i.e., over five pages)
	1.2. Identify if popular.	1.2.1. Check if the title of the article uses language for a general audience. 1.2.2. Check if the journal/magazine title is something you'd see on the newsstand. 1.2.3. Check if the length of the article is on the brief side.

2. Identify if my article is scholarly or popular.	2.1. Identify if scholarly.	2.1.1. Check if the article has a bibliography.
		2.1.2. Check expertise of the author (use handout).
		2.1.3. Check if the article has an abstract at the beginning.
	2.2. Identify if popular.	2.2.1. Check if the article does not have a bibliography.
		2.2.2. Check the expertise of the author (use handout).
		2.2.3. Check if the article does not have an abstract in the beginning.

After these kinds of discussions, it became apparent that it was unrealistic for the workshop to cover both tasks shown in the table in addition to the many other things that needed to be covered in the workshop. The team decided that task 1, "Identify if my citation is scholarly or popular," was the most important need-to-know item. The argument was that students were apt to make the popular or scholarly decision at the citation level, and that helping them make this an informed decision was critical. Task 2 was moved onto the nice-to-know list and was not taught in the workshop.

Note that task 1 would have reflected far more nuances and entailed far more knowledge if this has been written for a graduate student audience. This discussion helped us to define our learners and revisit our learner analysis data.

Are You All Set?

Have you

- ✔ Used your module groups to develop one (or only a few) tasks for each module?
- ✔ Broken down the tasks into subtasks and steps?
- ✔ Questioned your assumptions about what the learners know so that the steps are written to the appropriate levels?

Answer key for quiz on page 56

Click on File and then Save As. This is a step. We could assume that this learner group could accomplish this without any further task breakdown.

Tags are surrounded by the less than (<) and greater than (>) symbols. This is not a task, subtask, or step. This is a knowledge statement and will be addressed later in the design process.

Type in the name of your file: a:/xxxx.html. This is a step that would follow "Click on File and then Save As."

Review the page using Internet Explorer. This is probably a subtask for this particular learner group since they may need further help completing this item. With other learner groups, this item might be a step, not needing any more explanation.

Create a basic web page. This is the only task. All the other items on this list fall under this task.

Cascading style sheets are not required. Again, this is not a task, subtask, or step, but rather a knowledge statement and will be addressed later in the design process.

Save and name the file. This is probably a subtask for this learner group, necessitating a further breakdown into the steps shown above.

STEP 7

Create Teaching Points

Prior to this step, the focus has been on what learners will be *doing*—the tasks at which they need to be competent in order to meet their goals. In this step the design process starts to focus on what the learners need to *understand* in order to do the task well.

Teaching points are the essential pieces of knowledge that the learners must understand—the points that the learners must walk away with in order for the workshop to be successful. This will vary greatly with the goal of the workshop and the tasks necessary for completion. One designer might believe strongly, for example, that being exposed to and understanding key vocabulary is important to the learners' ultimate success and may design a teaching point that encapsulates aspects of this understanding: "A database record is divided into multiple fields," or "A citation contains information about the article such as the title, article name, magazine name, and author of the article." Given another workshop with different goals and audience, the same designer might think that this kind of information would fall under the nice-to-know category.

The key is that teaching points are carefully chosen, worded, and supported by the related task in such a way that a learner truly "gets it." And for that to happen, teaching points will need to be emphasized and reemphasized during the workshop. For optimal learning:

- Teaching points should be heard
- Teaching points should be read
- Teaching points should be discussed
- Understanding of the teaching points should be reflected in the ability of the learners to complete their tasks

CREATING TEACHING POINTS

Review the need-to-know list.

> Look for potential teaching points that did not fit into the task analysis. Do you still agree that these items are need-to-know items? Is there anything missing from the list? Keep asking, "What do the learners absolutely need to know to successfully complete their tasks?"

Review the needs assessment and learner analysis.

> Look for feedback that indicates the workshop should include background or theory.

Review the task analysis.

> Are there any tasks, subtasks, or steps that would be problematic if the learner did not know something in particular (such as the theory or history behind it)?

Choose judiciously.

> If you have too many teaching points per module (more than two to four), you may move your learners into a state of cognitive overload where they are not able to learn anything new (see step 4 for a review of this concept).

Test the teaching points

> Like the task analysis, teaching points are highly contextual. One learner group may understand the same teaching point that would leave another learner group in a cloud of confusion. Regardless of the target learners, sometimes the sentences that seem perfectly clear to a librarian may be very obscure and almost meaningless to the learners. It is preferable, therefore, that teaching points be tested on representatives from the learner group. It may work to simply approach current library users who fit the learner demographic, tell them the teaching point, and ask them to explain in their own words what it means. Make sure the teaching points are easy to understand when heard just once. If a teaching point needs explanation, it will be more difficult for the learners to comprehend and many might be left behind. Therefore, avoid jargon or confusing phrases. Be rigorous about each word, each phrase. Ask the learner "testers" how they might be confused or might misinterpret the teaching point. Look for furrowed brows, confused looks, and questions like, "What do you mean?" or "Can you say that again?" Those are the obvious signs that the teaching points need more work. Keep refining them. Go back to your representative learners and see if the points now work better. This refining process is especially important because the workshop design may use these teaching points frequently. They might be on flipcharts, on PowerPoint presentations, and on handouts. They might be repeated several times in each module, and they might end up in a tutorial if the designer chooses to create an online version of the workshop.

Checklist for Creating Good Teaching Points

Are any parts of the teaching points confusing to a learner?

Could a teaching point be misconstrued and interpreted in a misleading way?

Do any seem to be less critical? In other words, will the learners figure out this teaching point on their own during the workshop?

Are there ways to make the teaching points clearer so that they can be said aloud, but also be stand-alones on a handout or flipchart and still make perfect sense?

Try It Out

Look at the following potential teaching points. How do they fare given the preceding checklist?

An article index is where you find a list of articles that the library may or may not own.

Use ILL if the library doesn't have what you're looking for.

Citations contain information about the article.

Full text is the entire text of the article, not necessarily the photos or the graphs and charts.

Most tags are paired: a start tag < . . . > and an end tag </ . . . >.

Cascading style sheets are not required.

Again, depending on the learner group's prior knowledge and level, some of these teaching points may make perfect sense, while others may confound. Some may be misleading, less essential, or awkward to say aloud.

SUMMARY

So far in the design process we have focused on the things learners need to be able to *do* to be successful. This step shifts our focus to what learners need to *understand* in order to be successful. Teaching points will be used in many different ways, so careful consideration of their vocabulary and sentence structure during this step will pay off in future steps of the design process.

Case Study

The design team for the Unravel workshops struggled over teaching content items. Some designers felt it was important to include as many as six or seven teaching points per module, while others argued for just a couple. It was challenging to yet again sort through what was need-to-know and what was nice-to-know.

The wording of the points was also labored over. Do we call an index a *database* or an *article index* or a *periodical index* or just simply an *index*? Do we sometimes use the term *periodical* and other times *journal or magazine*? These sorts of inconsistencies had to be discussed and compromises had to be made so that our vocabulary would not further confuse our learners.

Likewise, the team questioned the uses of technical vocabulary. Was it important to use the term *Boolean* or should we just use AND, OR, and NOT connectors to mean *Boolean*? For what learner group would it be negligent not to use some level of library terminology, and for which group would it be highly advisable to do so?

The team also had to grapple over what terms really mean and how they could best be communicated. For example, in the Unravel 3: Advanced Searching workshop, which was designed to teach some of the "insider" tricks of the trade to upper-level undergraduates, the teaching points for a module on truncation and limiting were particularly difficult to formulate. What exactly is truncation? How can that be explained simply in one sentence or phrase? Think about the many ways one could respond to this question. The design team settled on two teaching points:

Truncation is a way to search for various forms of a word

There are different truncation and limiting features for most databases

Are You All Set?

Have you

- ✔ Reviewed previous steps in the design process for possible teaching points?
- ✔ Especially focused on pulling out teaching points from your need-to-know list?
- ✔ Identified other teaching points that would be essential for the learners to be able to complete each task?
- ✔ Tried out your teaching points on others for clarity?
- ✔ Refined them so that they can stand alone on a flipchart, handout, and so on?

STEP 8

Write Objectives

Some instructional design processes start by creating explicit objective statements. The process described in this book, however, works very gradually toward writing objectives. Everything that has come before will now serve as preparation for what becomes in large part an articulation of decisions already made. In fact, once the designer or team has identified and grouped the need-to-knows, created the task analyses, and settled on the teaching points, the objectives have practically written themselves. Creating objectives pulls together all of these content-related steps.

Note that in this chapter, objectives are often referred to as "learning" objectives. This is to help differentiate them from teaching objectives. As an example, a teaching objective might be "to demonstrate the difference between a keyword and a subject search." This is an objective written for the instructor. In contrast, a learning objective is written for the learner: "Given access to Academic Search Premier, find articles on the Vietnam War using both a keyword and a subject search."

WHY CREATE LEARNING OBJECTIVES?

They make explicit exactly what the learners will accomplish in each module of the workshop.

They make explicit how success will be judged. If the learners are able to show mastery of the objectives, then the workshop will be deemed successful. If the learners are not able to show mastery, then the workshop needs to be redesigned.

They become your promise to the client and learners as to what you will deliver in the workshop.

They can be used to advertise and market the workshops.

WRITING OBJECTIVES

Many librarians and staff have learned to write learning objectives in courses or workshops designed for teaching. What may be different in this process is that the emphasis here is on writing objectives for one-shot workshops in which the instructor's purview begins and ends with the workshop.

The objectives for one-shot workshops should

Focus on what the learners will be able to do or write or say during or by the end of the workshop

Avoid knowledge words such as "know" or "understand" that are harder to track in a one-shot workshop

Tell the learners what they should be able to accomplish after the workshop (e.g., "Given a list of journal names, use the e-journals page to identify journals that are available online") and *not* what the instructor should be doing (e.g., "Demonstrate using the e-journals page to find if a journal is online")

Identify the tool, criterion, or other method the learners will use to complete the objective (e.g., "given a list of journal names," or "given three criteria")

Give the designer a specific way to test if learning has occurred

Rules of Thumb for Writing Learning Objectives

The learning objectives for one-shot workshops are

- Behaviorally based (they cause behavior to be changed)
- Visual (you can see them being met)
- Measurable (you can measure if the learners met the standard or qualifier)

They also

- Use action verbs
- Stay away from knowledge or comprehension verbs

Learning objectives often include three parts: a condition under which the action takes place (shown here in bold), a task (shown in italic), and a qualifier or performance standard (shown underlined). For example,

Given a research topic and access to the library's home page, *find* <u>three relevant articles</u> *that the library owns*.

Using an article citation, *search the catalog* <u>to find if the library owns the journal</u>.

<table>
<tr><td colspan="2">*Tip*</td></tr>
<tr><td>Instead of saying . . .</td><td>Say . . .</td></tr>
<tr><td>know</td><td>write, define, repeat, name, list</td></tr>
<tr><td>understand</td><td>restate, describe, locate, access, illustrate</td></tr>
<tr><td>analyze</td><td>differentiate between/among, contrast</td></tr>
<tr><td colspan="2">*Source*: Adapted from Mel Silberman and Carol Auerbach, *Active Training: A Handbook of Techniques, Designs, Case Examples, and Tips* (Pfeiffer, 1988).</td></tr>
</table>

Given a research topic and an advanced search screen in the catalog, *combine search terms* <u>using the Boolean operators AND, OR, NOT</u>.

Notice how these three parts distinguish this way of writing learning objectives from other methods. For example, notice the differences between these two objectives:

"Students will be able to distinguish between a scholarly and a popular article."

"Given a list of citations, students will identify three factors that distinguish a popular article from a scholarly article."

The first objective sounds good, but leaves a lot to the imagination. Would the client, the learners, or other instructors be in agreement as to what it would look like if the learners were able to achieve this objective? How would the instructor measure the learners' progress toward meeting this objective?

The second objective, by contrast, is specific, clear, and measurable. It also gives the instructional designer enough information to move to the next steps in the design. For example, the first part, "Given a list of citations," tells the designer that the learners will be using a list of citations and not the sources themselves. The qualifier tells the designer that there will be at least three factors covered in the workshop. This will make step 9 in the design process (assessing whether the learners had achieved this objective) fairly straightforward: Can the learners identify three factors that indicate whether the citation they are using would lead to a scholarly or a popular article?

Using the Task Analysis to Write Learning Objectives

Do not start from scratch when writing learning objectives—you've already done a lot of this work. Every task in the task analysis can become the basis for an objective statement. Building from the task analysis in this way will make creating learning objectives one of the speediest parts of the design process.

Look again at the above examples. The central element of these objectives could be mapped directly to the task analysis. So, for example, if the task was to "Identify if my citation is scholarly or popular," all the designer needs to do is add the condition under which the action will be performed:

"Given a citation"

And then add the qualifier or performance standard:

"three factors"

Try It Out

Go back to your task analysis and identify three tasks from which to write learning objectives. Next, identify the condition and then the standard.

	Condition	Task (from task analysis)	Qualifier/standard
Example	Using Dreamweaver	create a basic web page	that includes text in two columns, a photo, and the library logo
Your turn			
Your turn			
Your turn			

Often this order (condition followed by task, followed by the qualifier or standard) works well for an objective, but in some cases, the objective flows better in a slightly different order. Once you have the three parts of the objective, you can reorder the parts in a way that makes sense, such as in this example:

> **Given a research topic and access to the library's home page,** *find* <u>three relevant</u> *articles* <u>that the library owns</u>.

IMPORTANCE OF OBJECTIVES

Well-articulated objectives can become the most visible and important part of the workshop. They are the deliverables that the client will count on the library workshop to produce. So when the library says that learners will be able to define an article index, locate three appropriate article indexes for a particular topic, and so on, the library is promising that learners will leave the workshop able to do those things. The client knows exactly what to expect from the workshop and later from the learners. It is our pact with the client, and it can be a powerful way for the library to sell its instruction program.

SUMMARY

Learning objectives communicate to the client, the learners, and other library staff exactly what the learners will be able to do at the completion of the workshop. The objectives are often taken from the task list and include a condition under which the task is performed (e.g., location, resources available, equipment used, etc.) and a measurable standard or qualifier (e.g., accuracy, quality, quantity, etc.).

Writing objectives was so far the simplest step of the design process for the University of Minnesota's Unravel design team. Most of the objective is very straightforward—a condition and an action. But the piece that was by far the most interesting was the standard or qualifier. Was it enough for the learners to just complete the task, or did it have to be completed to meet some kind of standard? What kind of standards would be measurable, observable, and straightforward? If we say that a task has to be done "correctly" will that mean the same thing to all the instructors? Will that mean the same thing to the learners and the client? What about the term *relevant*? To be honest, this discussion sometimes ended up in a black hole.

The goal, therefore, became to use a standard or qualifier only when it would be linked to an assessment or an exercise. If we could see that the qualifier was fulfilled (for example, that the students identified three article indexes in a specific discipline), then we kept it in the objective statement. Otherwise, we settled for merely a completion of a task ("Construct a record using preidentified fields").

Another way we used learning objectives was to clearly distinguish between the various components of the lesson plan. So, for example, if a library instructor wants to teach how to identify an appropriate index, she can easily locate which module of the workshop delivers that objective. She can also quickly see what kind of condition and what kind of performance standard the lesson plan covers. She can then focus on changing the pieces of the lesson plan that relate to the condition or performance standard she wants to adjust, given the level of the target learners or other unique factors.

Are You All Set?

Have you

- ✔ Started to write the objectives using the tasks from the task analysis?
- ✔ Added in a condition under which each task will be done?
- ✔ Added in a qualifier or performance standard that is behavioral, measurable, and testable?

Build Evaluation Tools

Because the library is promising to deliver on the learning objectives designed in the previous step, the designer has to have some way to determine that the objectives are in fact being met. Step 9 in the design process is about creating the tools that will do just that. Evaluation tools can also give the designer feedback on how the learners perceived the workshop, how effective the workshop may have been at improving the learners' application of what they learned, and if this ultimately made a difference in their overall success. In other words, did the workshop live up to the needs identified in the needs assessment conducted in step 1?

KIRKPATRICK'S LEVELS OF EVALUATION

Although there are several different models for evaluation, Donald Kirkpatrick offers training professionals what is often called *the* definitive evaluation framework. Kirkpatrick covers four different levels at which to evaluate the effectiveness of a workshop:

Level 1: Reaction evaluation

Asks: Did they *like* it?

Level 2: Learning evaluation

Asks: Did they *get* it?

Level 3: Behavioral evaluation

Asks: Do they *apply* it?

Level 4: Results evaluation

Asks: Does it make a *difference*?

We will examine each of these levels of evaluation in detail.

LEVEL 1: REACTION EVALUATION

The most basic evaluation feedback is a reaction evaluation. These evaluations are basically perception surveys that seek to learn what the learners thought about the workshop. Did they like it? Did they think they learned anything from the workshop? What did they think about the presenter's style? Were they comfortable?

Reaction evaluations may use Likert Scales or multiple-choice and open-ended questions. There are countless examples of reaction evaluation questions. W. Leslie Rae, a prolific author on the topic of learning evaluations, suggests the ones shown in figure 9-1.

> ### Tip
>
> Kirkpatrick's four levels of evaluation have been widely adopted in the training field. To learn more about Kirkpatrick's model, see his book *Evaluating Training Programs: The Four Levels*, now in its second edition (Berrett-Koehler, 1998). If you need to include return on investment in your evaluation strategy, Jack Phillip adds a fifth level to Kirkpatrick's model in the book *Return on Investment in Training and Performance Improvement Programs*, also in its second edition (Butterworth Heinemann, 2003).

FIGURE 9-1 Sample reaction evaluation questions

To what extent do you feel you have learned from the workshop?

> *Learned a lot*　6　5　4　3　2　1　*Learned nothing*

If you circled 6, 5, or 4 please describe

> (a) what you have learned and
>
> (b) what you intend to do with this learning (on your return to work/ in your course/etc.)

If you circled 3, 2, or 1, what were the reasons you gave this rating?

To what extent do you feel you have had previous learning (perhaps including some you have forgotten) confirmed?

> *Confirmed a lot*　6　5　4　3　2　1　*Confirmed little*

If you circled 6, 5, or 4, please describe

> (a) what has been confirmed and
>
> (b) what you intend to do with this learning (on your return to work/ in your course/etc.)

If you circled 3, 2, or 1, please state as fully as possible the reasons why you gave this rating.

What have you not learned that you needed to and/or expected to learn during the workshop? Please describe fully any items.

Although easy to make, distribute, and analyze, there are many limitations with this kind of evaluation. For example, it is difficult to separate satisfaction with the training itself from satisfaction with non-training components such as the sense of humor of the instructor or the donuts and coffee provided. This "halo effect" can affect how learners respond on a variety of more substantive measures that have nothing to do with donuts or jokes.

The most glaring limitation with reaction evaluations is that there is no clear link between the likeability of the workshop and the degree of learning that occurred. In other words, a learner could have disliked the workshop and the presenter, but still have met the learning objectives.

Consider, however, the implications for subsequent offerings of the same or even different library workshops if a substantial number of learners dislike the workshop. Learners who are part of a community of learners (such as in a certain major, club, or group) may spread their negative reaction among the group, cautioning others against attending library workshops. Disgruntled learners may also give the client negative feedback, dissuading him or her from sending future learners to library workshops. Gathering reaction evaluations with a pilot group of learners, or early on in the offering of the workshop, may help the design team improve future offerings of the workshop and limit negative public relations down the road.

There can be several other useful outcomes from a reaction evaluation:

Learners' responses may be helpful in future advertising of the workshop.

Sharing responses with the client may maintain that client's interest in the workshop.

The responses may also play a role in enhancing learner retention of a concept, skill, or knowledge they gained in the workshop. Remember, just the act of writing down what the learner has learned in a reaction evaluation helps that learner retain that item.

LEVEL 2: LEARNING EVALUATION

Reaction evaluations are helpful at revealing what the learners thought about the workshop, but how can the design team find out if the learners have truly learned anything in the workshop? The learning evaluation is mapped directly to the objectives and teaching points developed previously in the design process. This is the kind of evaluation we are most familiar with—a knowledge or performance test—during which the learners demonstrate what they have learned. Let's look at both of these types separately.

> **Tip**
>
> Sometimes the reaction evaluation is also called a "smile sheet" because it was common to use smiley faces in the measurement scales.

> **Tip**
>
> There are many more examples of questions available at http://www.businessballs.com/trainingevaluationtools.pdf. A reaction evaluation is also included in the case study at the end of this chapter.

Performance Test

A performance test challenges the learners to apply the skills they have learned to an actual situation. The most effective performance test pulls the entire workshop together and asks students to engage in an activity that reflects their real-world situation (some readers may recognize this as something called a criterion test). This would challenge the learners to integrate their new skills and knowledge and apply it in their actual situation. For example, the last part of a workshop on conducting company research in preparation for a job interview might be devoted to a final assignment during which each learner is given a company's name and time to research that company (individually, in pairs, or in teams) and to complete a short worksheet that reflects the key areas covered in the workshop. The library instructor would circulate, assess the learning, and coach the learners as needed.

This would be ideal. But often there is simply not enough time either during the workshop or later for the instructor to give such an extensive performance test. Instead of asking learners to complete the entire research process as taught, the learners may be asked to complete just a piece of it. You've already designed the basic skeleton for this approach during the last step of the design process: creating learning objectives. The learning objective merely needs to be reworked into a performance question that can stand on its own when used with the learners. For example:

If the objective reads . . .	The performance question may read . . .
Given a research topic and access to the library's home page, find three relevant articles that the library owns.	Using the library's home page, find three articles on the topic of affirmative action in higher education and identify which library these articles are in.
Using an article citation, search the catalog to find if the library owns a certain journal.	Search the catalog for the citations listed below and identify which library you would find the item in or indicate if the library does not own the item.

Once the performance questions have been identified, creating the worksheet or testing sheet can be done very quickly. In many circumstances, these worksheets may be integrated into step 13 and a traditional end-of-class skills test may be eliminated. (See the next chapter for discussion of this strategy.)

Knowledge Test

For many instructors, administering and analyzing a performance test as outlined above is simply an unrealistic time investment. Given this, a knowledge test may be the best-case scenario. Knowledge testing is the kind of assessment that librarians and students are most familiar with. Although rather difficult to craft, once finished, the questions can be used and reused in a variety of workshops. Quantifiable test questions are very easy to grade and analyze, and qualitative (open-ended) questions do not have to create a great deal of work.

Each question on the test should be mapped directly to a particular module of the workshop. Teaching points and objectives can provide the basis of each question, as shown in figure 9-2.

The results can be extremely helpful in assessing the effectiveness of both the instructor and the lesson plan. If many learners get a particular answer incorrect, the designer knows there is a problem with the workshop. The designer and the instructors would then need to diagnose the root cause of the incorrect answer.

FIGURE 9-2   Sample knowledge test

Objective	Teaching Point	Test Question
Using an article citation, search the catalog to find if the library owns a journal.	Need to search the catalog for the name of the magazine, journal, or newspaper rather than the article title. Why? Because articles are not included in the catalog.	In the library catalog, I need to search by the _____ to find out if the library has the article I want. a. title of the article b. name of the journal/ magazine/newspaper c. author of the article d. any of these
Given a list of citations, identify three factors that distinguish a popular article from a scholarly article.	Examine the intended audience of a journal or magazine to help distinguish between scholarly and popular sources. Popular sources are written for generalists; scholarly sources are written for experts and academics in a particular field.	_____ articles are normally written for experts in a particular field. a. Popular b. Scholarly c. Citations of d. Journal or magazine

Incorrect Answer Diagnosis

What happens when the learners consistently get a question wrong? Look for the following three problems.

Test Problem

Is the test question the problem? Is the wording of the question or the possible answers confusing? Are any of the possible answers misleading? Could more than one of the possible answers be correct? Writing effective test questions is a challenge, even for full-time teachers who must do so all the time. Library instructional designers of knowledge tests may need to test the questions ahead of time with representative target learners or consult with educational specialists.

Delivery Problem

Is the instructor digressing from the lesson plan in a way that is not meeting the particular learning objective? Can the instructor pinpoint the problem and eliminate that behavior in future workshops? If so, did that address the problem? On the flip side, there may be an instructor who consistently gets stellar results on her tests. These "deviations" from the lesson plan could be standardized for future instructors.

Instructional Design Problem

Is the problem due to some aspect of the lesson plan that the question corresponds to? Is there adequate skills practice in the module in question? Are learners getting the feedback they need to adjust their skills and knowledge during this module? Are the teaching points not getting through to the learners? See steps 15 and 16 for further discussion of various aspects of the lesson plan that might be useful in additional diagnosis.

LEVEL 3: BEHAVIORAL EVALUATION

Assessing the reactions of the learners and their ability to accomplish a skill or remember a piece of new knowledge directly after the workshop is at best a limited measure of actual learning. What most librarians are concerned about is whether the attainment of the learning objectives changed the learners' ultimate behavior. Go back to the client's definition of success from step 1. These definitions are most likely focused on getting the learners to do something differently or do it better than they had before. Did the learners use scholarly sources for their final papers? Did the learners successfully research a company and use that information in their next interview? Did the learners implement their learning into the next web pages they designed?

In other words, after all the learning, did the learners end up doing anything differently? Did they do it well? This kind of evaluation needs to be tied in closely with the client's ultimate outcome for the learners. Therefore, the design team will need to work closely with the client on an effective way to evaluate the learner.

There are countless possibilities for designing a behavioral evaluation:
The client could add specific criteria to their final paper or project's scoring rubric that would evaluate a key learning objective for the library workshop. The results would then be shared with the library instructor and designer.

The client could require a research journal or offer the learners an incentive to complete a research journal which the librarian scores.

The librarian could administer a self-assessment survey to the client on their perception of behavioral changes based on the learners' subsequent performance.

The librarian or the client could administer a self-assessment survey to the learners in order to understand the level of behavioral changes they perceive they made.

Designing Grading Rubrics

In K–12 and higher education, the design team will often need to create a grading rubric for the level-3 evaluation. Grading rubrics break down learner performance into components and can be designed to point to specific modules of the workshop that need improvement. They can work with a finished project or with a research journal.

To create a rubric, list the workshop objectives on the left-hand side. Then create a range of performance indicators that would illustrate the degree of attainment of the objectives. These go along the top as criteria and are assigned a point value. The example in figure 9-3 shows just one objective and the points assigned for degree of aptitude in achieving the objective.

In order to analyze the data, the designer would look for patterns. Are the majority of students scoring a low number for a particular objective? This may indicate that the corresponding part of the workshop needs further attention. If, on the other hand, scores are high for a particular module, this may indicate that the module is successful and needs no further attention.

For many in libraries, applying an entire grading rubric to library research may be the exception to the norm. In these cases, if the client is using a grading rubric, they may be amenable to adding a library component to theirs. If, for example, the client is most concerned with the quality of information used in a project, they might add one dimension on quality to their own grading rubric.

FIGURE 9-3   **Sample grading rubric for a behavioral evaluation**

Workshop Objective	Criteria				Points
	1	2	3	4	
Given a research topic and access to the library's home page, find three relevant articles that the library owns.	Learner was not able to use the library's home page to find articles.	Learner used the library's home page but was unsucessful at using a library index to find articles.	Learner found one or two on-target articles in a library index.	Learner found three on-target articles in a library index.	

LEVEL 4: RESULTS EVALUATION

All the evaluation types discussed so far are just dabbling at what is really the bottom line—did the workshop make any overall difference? This level of evaluation addresses the big picture. The designer must identify what it is that truly matters not only to the client, but even beyond. What are the larger measures of success for the learners? In higher education it might be retention and a four-year graduation rate. In business it might be sales, market share, quality, or customer service. Look back to the needs assessment step and identify critical baseline measures for the client. Then compare the success figures from before and after the workshop.

The most obvious issue with this level of evaluation is that it is highly unrealistic for measuring a single workshop—even if this workshop is offered many times. Alternatively, the designer can identify smaller "bottom lines" such as overall course grades, satisfaction rates of students in a particular program, or results of a particular question posed on an institutional survey. Again, identify a baseline measure (from prior to the workshop) against which to measure the perceived impact of the workshop or instruction program.

EVALUATION PLAN WORKSHEET

When planning an overall evaluation strategy, think about the various ways to time each evaluation. It may be helpful to fill in the worksheet in figure 9-4 to help organize the evaluation process.

FIGURE 9-4   Evaluation plan worksheet

Type of Evaluation	Before Workshop	During Workshop	After Workshop
Level 1: Reaction			
Level 2: Learning			
Performance Test			
Knowledge Test			
Level 3: Behavioral			
Level 4: Results			

SUMMARY

Once the task analysis, teaching points, and learning objectives are complete, the designer begins to create the tools used to evaluate the success of the workshop. There are four different ways to evaluate a workshop: measure what learners liked and didn't like about the workshop; measure if the learners learned what you taught them; measure if the learners can apply what they learned to their own work; and measure if it actually made a difference in the ultimate success of the learners.

Case Study

The Unravel design team at the University of Minnesota started with level-1 and level-2 evaluations. These were manageable levels that the library could administer without too much work and that would provide important formative data for subsequent workshop designs.

LEVEL 1: REACTION EVALUATION

Workshop pilots all started with a level-1 reaction evaluation with the pilot group and were continued with the actual workshop participants. Figure 9-5 shows the actual form used.

After several rounds of collecting this data, the design team felt that it had gotten enough feedback on these measures and decided to swap out this evaluation for a more open-ended optional feedback sheet, shown in figure 9-6.

LEVEL 2: LEARNING EVALUATION

The Unravel design team designed a knowledge test that is still, several years later, being improved. A subteam would write a quiz question that the rest of the design team thought was okay—until after receiving all the quiz results. Then the team would realize that either the question or the answers were confusing. If you can't trust the quiz question, it's hard to trust the results.

For example, one of the most difficult things to get across to students is that they can't find articles in the OPAC (in this case called "MNCAT"). The quiz question that covers this used to read:

> In MNCAT, I need to search by the _____ to find out if the University of Minnesota Libraries own the article I want.
>
> a. title of the article
>
> b. title of the journal/magazine/newspaper
>
> c. author of the article
>
> d. any of these

Some members of the design team felt that the question itself was too confusing and that this contributed to the poor results from this question. They were happier with the simpler, revised version. Note too the change from first person to second:

> To find out if the University of Minnesota Libraries own the article you want, you need to search by the _____ in MNCAT.

The same four possible responses are then listed as above.

Figure 9-7 on page 80 shows one of the later versions of the quiz.

FIGURE 9-5   Unravel 1 workshop level 1 evaluation form

YOUR STATUS: (circle)

1st year   2nd year   upperclass   grad   faculty   staff   non-affiliate

1. I found this workshop to be

UNINTERESTING	1	2	3	4	5	INTERESTING
WORTHLESS	1	2	3	4	5	VALUABLE
TOO SLOW	1	2	3	4	5	TOO FAST
PASSIVE	1	2	3	4	5	ACTIVE
TOO EASY	1	2	3	4	5	TOO DIFFICULT
IRRELEVANT	1	2	3	4	5	RELEVANT
DISORGANIZED	1	2	3	4	5	ORGANIZED
INFLEXIBLE	1	2	3	4	5	FLEXIBLE
BAD	1	2	3	4	5	GOOD
TENSE	1	2	3	4	5	RELAXED

2. This session completely met my expectations.

DISAGREE	1	2	3	4	5	AGREE

3. If your expectations were not completely met, please note expectations not met.

4. Which *three* things about this workshop did you find most useful?

5. How could this workshop be improved? Content? Delivery? Handouts?

6. Other comments?

FIGURE 9-6   Unravel 2 workshop optional feedback form

What is one thing you learned today that you think will be useful?

What is one thing you didn't know about the library before this session?

What is one thing you'd share with someone about what you learned?

Do you have any other comments or feedback?

FIGURE 9-7   Unravel 2 workshop level 2 evaluation quiz

HOW WELL DID WE TEACH YOU?

1. _____ is good to use to help you select article indexes with different perspectives (i.e., business or environment).

    a. Assignment Calculator   c. an article index
    b. Research QuickStart   d. LUMINA

2. Searching in _____ will give you a list of articles that have been published on your topic.

    a. an article index   c. a library catalog
    b. MNCAT   d. the Assignment Calculator

3. A good starting place to search for articles on your topic is in _____.

    a. subject headings   c. Expanded Academic Index
    b. MNCAT   d. a library catalog

4. Some article indexes provide the _____ of the article, while some only give you the citation of the article.

    a. record   c. subject
    b. full text   d. index

5. To find out if the University of Minnesota Libraries own the article you want, you need to search by the _____ in MNCAT.

    a. title of the article   c. author of the article
    b. name of the journal/magazine/newspaper   d. any of these

6. To find out what is owned by the U of M Libraries, you should search _____.

    a. LUMINA   c. MNCAT
    b. Expanded Academic Index   d. Research QuickStart

7. To locate a book or journal/magazine/newspaper in the library at the U of M, you will need the _____.

    a. call number   c. library name
    b. location in library   d. all of these

8. _____ articles are normally written for experts in a particular field.

    a. scholarly   c. popular
    b. journal   d. citations of

Congratulations!

You have unraveled the research process.

Now get out there and practice, practice, practice. Ask questions when you have them to further build your knowledge, and consider taking the next workshop in the series, Unravel 3: Advanced Searching.

Are You All Set?

Have you

- ✔ Chosen the types of evaluations you will use (levels 1, 2, 3, and 4)?
- ✔ Worked with the client (if applicable) to design the types of evaluations you choose?
- ✔ Designed the evaluations such as a self-assessment survey for the learners or client, a test, or a grading rubric?
- ✔ Piloted test questions to reveal problems ahead of time (if applicable)?

STEP 10
Create Checks for Understanding

With even the best teachers, only a modest amount of learning can occur in the 50–90 minute time frame commonly allocated to one-shot workshops. If a learner gets lost at any point in this short time period and gives up on learning, the library and the library instructor have lost a valuable opportunity. By the time the instructor is able to review the evaluations after the workshop, it's often too late to rescue the situation.

This step ensures that the instructional designer builds in ways to frequently monitor learning throughout the workshop. These "checks for understanding" allow the instructor to quickly assess what the learners are learning and how well they are learning (or not learning, as the case may be). This is true formative feedback from which the instructor gets the information she needs to take immediate action to remedy the situation if necessary.

Do not confuse a check for understanding with a way to compensate for a weak workshop design. Instead, think of it as a way to find individuals who might be lost otherwise or those individuals who have simply given up in their confusion and have stopped learning. If the workshop was designed well, the majority of learners should pass the check with flying colors. That said, in the real world it is possible to teach the very same workshop to the same kind of learners with different levels of success. The check for understanding can help the instructor make minor adjustments that could make the difference between a mediocre and a successful learning experience.

Most instructors build in informal checks for understanding by posing a question to the class and having one or two students respond. Others are able to read body language and make inferences from this. These are fine techniques and are often very useful, but they do not serve as a substitute for an adequate check for understanding. It is not enough to know that the one student in the class who answered the question has an understanding of the content—the check for understanding should provide avenues for every student to give that assurance. In this way the instructor can help ensure that each student is fulfilling the learning objectives and will be successful in the final learner evaluation.

There is an additional benefit from designing checks for understanding when working with unmotivated students or those required to attend; it is often at this point that they realize that they are expected to not only pay attention, but to work during the workshop period. School-aged students—and even those years beyond school—tend to be socialized to perform when a situation resembles a pop quiz or a performance in front of peers, as checks for understanding tend to do. This does wonders for waking up students and getting them engaged with the material.

> *Some students will look a little flustered when you check for understanding. You will see them panic a little, and scramble to find the right answers. This is good. It means they have awakened from sleeping with their eyes open, and that they will pay attention for a little while. Make sure you implement these checks. It will be good for your students and make you a much more effective instructor.*
>
> —Debra Payne Chaparro, PhD Student and Teaching Assistant, University of Minnesota Libraries–Twin Cities

DESIGNING A CHECK FOR UNDERSTANDING

A check for understanding should give the instructor *tangible evidence* that the students have achieved some kind of understanding. Gazing out across the computer lab and seeing people typing on the computer would not be considered tangible evidence of learning. Being able to see that the students have written correct answers on a worksheet would be.

A check for understanding occurs for each task or group of teaching points covered in the workshop. It might consist of the completion of a task or a quick response to a question mapped to a teaching point. The students would be asked to respond to the task or question on a worksheet. For example, if the task is to identify whether the library has a particular book, the check for understanding might be for students to look up a book and write down the call number for that book. If there are a group of teaching points, the check for understanding might be a series of fill-in-the-blank or multiple-choice questions. To check if the students have "gotten it," the instructor and assistant might walk up and down the aisles, making sure the correct answer is written, and if not, helping the students with their specific problems.

In situations when an assistant instructor is not available to help with the workshop, students might be asked to check their neighbor's answer, come to one shared answer, and write that down on their worksheets. The instructor then would only check each pair's response.

Another way to flag a potential learning problem is to give learners colored cards labeled A, B, C, D or yes and no (labeled on both sides of the card). Questions would be multiple choice and learners are asked to hold up their answers using the appropriate response card. In this way the instructor can quickly scan the class to see if there are any widespread problems and, hopefully, correct them before the workshop ends. Learners who answered correctly could be asked to explain why they answered that way, and then the instructor could reinforce the correct answer. Later in the workshop, the same question might be asked again and the instructor would check to see if the learners now appear to understand.

Although this method does not take much time, more thorough checks for understanding—such as those that involve having learners complete a task or sub-task and then recording their answers—take time, and time is precious in a one-shot workshop. Because of this, the designer might decide that the checks for understanding designed here will "double" as an "application" that will be covered in steps 12 and 13. This will ultimately save some of the precious workshop time.

PROCESS FOR CREATING CHECKS FOR UNDERSTANDING

Figure out exactly what learners would need to demonstrate to the instructor in order to show how well they are learning and how much they are learning.

Review the Evaluation Tools Created in the Last Step

Pay particular attention to the level-1 (reaction), level-2 (learning), and level-3 (behavioral) evaluations that were already designed. Are there pieces or entire parts of these evaluations that can be used as a check for understanding?

Review the Learning Objective and Teaching Points

Can the learning objective be broken down into short checks for understanding? Can a teaching point be tested in a check for understanding?

Design the Check for Understanding

Use the list in figure 10-1 for ways to design checks for understanding.

For more ideas, see *Classroom Assessment Techniques: A Handbook for College Teachers*, by Thomas Angelo and Patricia Cross (published by Jossey-Bass, 1993).

WHAT IF THEY DON'T UNDERSTAND?

Checks for understanding are designed to uncover places where a learner is stuck and just doesn't get it. This is a good thing—it means the instructor can remove what is in the way of the learner learning and pave the way to more understanding. It means the instructor can emphasize certain things and give attention to

FIGURE 10-1 Sample checks for understanding

Technique	Example on Worksheet
Subtask or step completion	Locate the page that allows you to order a book that is not at this library and write the URL here: _____

Multiple-choice questions	Given this citation, what would you type in to find if the library had this in its collection:
	
	    a. title of article
	    b. author
	    c. title of journal

Fill-in-the-blank questions	To find articles on my topic I would look in _____.
Approximate analogies: The learner completes the last part of an analogy.	A library catalog is to books as an index is to _____.
Problem scenarios: The learner reads a brief problem scenario and decides what to do.	The Boolean "OR" is to "more" as "AND" is to _____. You need to find census data. Using the library's website, find a web page with a link to census data and write the URL here: _____

those individuals who need it. But what about the possibility that a check for understanding uncovers little or no understanding among the majority of learners? What then?

In this case something may have gone wrong in the instructional design. Perhaps there was not time to do a proper needs assessment or learner analysis and the content was pitched at too high a level for the learners. Perhaps the designer had to skimp on time for a task analysis or teaching points or kept too many need-to-knows in the workshop, causing cognitive overload. These things happen. Before discovering these problems in front of a real live audience, there is still a chance to catch potential design problems in the workshop pilot. There are several ways to pilot a workshop. Skip ahead to step 16 to find out more.

SUMMARY

Checks for understanding give instructors the feedback they need to make quick adjustments to the workshop design if necessary or to focus in on those learners who need the most assistance. There are a number of techniques that can be intentionally incorporated into a workshop design to provide this feedback. These "checks for understanding" may be portions of the workshop evaluations created in the last step or pieces of the task analysis, teaching points, or learning objectives.

Case Study

Since the Unravel design team was working within the parameters of a short one-time workshop, for the most part we chose to use the application phases of the workshop as checks for understanding. As mentioned earlier, application will be covered in steps 12 and 13, but for the time being think of this as a check for understanding that doubles as a way to practice the material. Merging the check and the application allows the learners to spend more time learning the content than they might have if there were a separate check and a separate application.

Although we merged the two most of the time, in one case we did design in a rather quick and dirty check for understanding technique to see if learners could make good decisions between popular and scholarly resources. In this segment the instructor says a few sentences about the importance of using scholarly resources in college. Immediately following this brief introduction, learners are asked to read a handout that provides some distinguishing characteristics between popular and scholarly sources (this is the "presentation" phase, as you will learn in step 12). An attached worksheet asks them to read article citations and abstracts and "vote" on whether or not the items are scholarly or popular (this is the application phase covered in step 12). Then the instructor checks for understanding by having learners vote with a show of hands as to whether they think each item is popular, scholarly, or unsure. The instructor tallies the votes on the white board and then interjects presentation content for each item in order to reinforce four teaching points. These teaching points identify the ways first-year students can distinguish between a citation or an abstract that indicates the source is popular, scholarly, or part of the gray literature. These teaching points relate to length of article, vocabulary, audience, and availability of source.

Although this check for understanding is brief and easy to do, it requires each student to make a decision and reveal that decision through a show of hands. This allows the instructor to quickly assess how many students are having difficulty with the material. This then informs the instructor how much the teaching points should be reinforced during voting for the second, third, and fourth citation/abstract items.

The downside to this technique is having the students make a public announcement to the rest of the class. The design team has discussed a less intrusive process that would involve laminated cards marked P and S. Each student would get these cards and be asked to hold them up. This way everyone holds up their hands at once and no one is singled out as being right or wrong.

Are You All Set?

Have you

- ✔ Reviewed the tasks, subtasks, steps, teaching points, and learning objectives?
- ✔ Used this review to identify what immediate feedback you need to ensure that the learners are learning what's important?
- ✔ Reviewed techniques for the checks for understanding?
- ✔ Designed checks that ensure that *all* students can provide you with proof of their understanding?

STEP 11

Revisit the Need-to-Knows

This step marks the end of the first two phases in the instructional design process. At this point the designers will have assessed client needs and learner requirements, and have grappled intently with content issues. This is now a good time to revisit the need-to-know list developed in steps 3 and 4.

What you need:

- The need-to-know list
- The nice-to-know list
- The task analysis
- The teaching points
- The learning objectives

> You think you can just add in this or add that to the workshop, but those things always take more time than you think. And you don't know if the students are absorbing all of that. It just becomes a big mush of too much. I still fall into doing that sometimes—saying "and this and this and this"—but I'm way more aware of it than I used to be.
>
> —Malaika Grant, Reference and Instruction Librarian, University of Minnesota Libraries–Twin Cities

Take a look at all of these documents together. Are there any items in the task analysis that will be covered in the workshop that do not appear on the need-to-know list? What about any teaching points? Notice if some items on the nice-to-know list have crept back into the design. If so and if this is really what was intended, make these changes transparent by moving these items back to the need-to-know list. Conversely, notice if there are items on the need-to-know list that are not being used in the design and make those adjustments on the list.

QUESTIONS TO ASK

Once there is a complete, accurate list of the need-to-know items, there is another opportunity to filter the list down to the essentials.

Do all of the documents now support each other? Are there any contradictions left?

Does the need-to-know list still adequately reflect the instructional designer's intentions?

Is everything on the list still on-target for what the designer is trying to achieve?

Do the need-to-knows remaining on the list still look like a reasonable amount of material given time constraints?

Are there *any* items that could be moved to the nice-to-know list?

SUMMARY

This is a good time to make sure that the need-to-know list is still applicable and that the workshop design is still staying true to the original list. If this is not the case, the designer has an opportunity at this step to revisit the list and make adjustments to realign all the pieces of the workshop design created so far.

Case Study

The Unravel design team found that nice-to-knows would sometimes creep into subsequent steps such as teaching points and task analysis. In fact, this discussion was almost circular. The team would decide that finding a known book or article was going to be a nice-to-know for this particular workshop, yet several meetings later someone would reintroduce the idea and another discussion would ensue on the merits of this item. Taking better notes of these meetings would have helped, but in lieu of good notes, we had to cobble together historical discussions each time we circled back to a nice-to-know item.

In some cases these nice-to-know items that had either crept back into discussion or had appeared in a task analysis or objective were eventually put on a handout. E-mailing citations was a good example of this. Several team members could not let this item remain a nice-to-know, and an impasse led to the item being included on a handout.

Are You All Set?

Have you

✔ Combed through the task analysis, teaching points, and learning objectives for any additional need-to-know items that were not on the original list but should be included?

✔ Found any items on the need-to-know list that were not used in the task analysis, teaching points, and objectives?

✔ Made difficult decisions to further refine the final need-to-know list?

✔ Changed any documents that relate to this refining process?

Brainstorm Teaching Methods

So far in the instructional design process, the designer has focused on the assessment and content areas of the workshop. It is now time to consider the delivery of this content. This chapter explores how workshop content might be presented and how learners might get an opportunity to master the content.

This can be a challenging step. It involves some experimentation and risk-taking. Admittedly, it can be easier and more comforting to rely on the common classroom formula—start with a lecture, follow it with a demonstration, and then finish with hands-on activity. Sometimes this formula is conducted only once in an entire workshop; other times the instructor might use the formula several times throughout the same workshop. But there is a much wider repertoire of techniques to draw from that are more engaging and effective for the learners. The designer and instructors may start slowly by choosing just one or two new techniques to augment the lecture–demo–hands-on approach. Others may decide to fully replace their former approaches with totally new ones.

> ## Tip
>
> One of the most highly respected trainers of trainers, Bob Pike, says, "In our programs, we use the 90/20/8 rule. No module that we teach ever runs more than 90 minutes, the pace changes every 20 minutes, and we try to involve people in the content every eight minutes."
>
> —Robert Pike, *Creative Training Techniques Handbook: Tips, Tactics, and How-To's for Delivering Effective Training* (Lakewood, 1992).

HOW WE LEARN BEST

Before delving into techniques, it is helpful to have at least a basic understanding of how people learn. This chapter provides brief coverage of this topic. Although this cannot fully suffice, it is intended to provide at a minimum some justification for moving beyond the lecture–demo–hands-on formula.

Try It Out

Think about something that you learned very well. It could be the time you were taught to drive or play the recorder. Perhaps it was when you learned a new language or studied Nietzsche or Adam Smith. Whatever it was, think about that learning experience. What was it that set it out from more mundane learning experiences?

Your peak learning experience	What sets it apart?

Did the learning change:

How you think?

How you do things now?

The choices you now make?

Effective learning actually *changes* the learner. Even more effective learning *transforms* the learner. Was this your experience?

Next, think about what happened during this peak learning experience:

Did you watch others do something and develop your ideas based on that?

Did you immediately get involved and want to practice and practice until you got it? Then, did you learn the theory behind what you were doing?

Did you study the theory and use this to solve a problem or make a decision?

Was information presented to you in an organized way by an expert?

Was the learning opportunity structured or unstructured?

What question did you most often ask while you were learning?

- What is there to know?
- What if?
- Why not?
- How does this work?
- Why is this relevant?

Your responses to these questions begin to pinpoint how you learn best.

HOW WE ALL LEARN

If you sat in a randomly selected group to have a discussion about the preceding questions, you might notice how emphatic people can be about what they know about learning. It is common to project one's own particular learning style on to the learners. Sometimes one's own style becomes "the right way" to teach and the instructor adheres rigidly to that style in their workshops.

Also, it is equally interesting to notice those who continue using the lecture–demo–hands-on formula even though they personally do not learn best that way and would actually dislike being in their own class! You can bet that if they themselves do not learn best that way and if their peak learning experiences are very different from their own teaching approaches, they are failing to reach at least some of the learners in their workshop. By ignoring the different ways that learners learn best, we leave these learners behind.

The important and obvious lesson is that there are many ways that people learn best and no one way is "the right way." The caveat is that librarians who teach specialists or upper-level and graduate students may notice that these learners have self-selected into a discipline that has a particular learning style which is comfortable for them. For example, someone who learns best by reading, thinking, and developing theories may be drawn to disciplines for which that is a primary way of learning (e.g., philosophy or history). Another person who learns best by experimentation might be repelled by those fields but drawn to the lab sciences.

The bottom line is that if we are going to spend day after day in front of a classroom teaching hundreds of students, we need to know as much as we can about how people learn best and what we need to do as teachers to enable that to happen.

There should be some useful information in the learner analysis (step 2) that will help with this step. This information may show that the learners are too diverse to pigeonhole into a predominant learning style. Or there may be an indication that the discipline into which the learners have self-selected will allow for a narrower approach to selecting teaching methods. This is a great start.

Next the designer should have some basic cognitive psychology under his or her belt.

INFORMATION OVERLOAD

Try It Out

Think about where you are right now. What do you see around the edges of this book as you read? What do you hear? What does the seat feel like against your body? What do your clothes feel like against your body? What is the taste in your mouth? What does it feel like to breathe?

Given all that is going on in your environment right now, think about how much of this information you were aware of as you've been reading this book: 5 percent? 10 percent? 25 percent? 40 percent? 60 percent? More?

Human Filters

Most likely you filtered out the information that did not seem important to you at the time (e.g., the taste in your mouth and the way your clothes feel against your body) and were focusing on the content of this book. This is one of the remarkable things about human beings! There are potentially millions of pieces of information we might take in at any given time in our environment, but humans are endowed with great information filters. How much gets our attention? Only a fraction.

Human biology protects us from this onslaught of information. First, think about the five senses. At any given moment there are things to see, hear, smell, touch, and taste. That's a lot of sensory information. But all senses do not work equally. Human biology has set up a kind of hierarchy of the senses so that some of them are especially keen, and others are extremely limited. To see this, fill out the exercise in figure 12-1, and then look at the correct answers beneath it.

Expecting that students take in most of their information through hearing contradicts human biology. This data creates a powerful argument to fully leverage the power of sight to help students learn.

Now add to this data the discussion of peak learning experiences in the beginning of this chapter. Prominent and preferred learning styles can also serve as a filter. For example, how many students "tune out" the lecture, but become very engaged during a hands-on activity? Learners will often filter out information that comes to them in a way that they cannot process well.

The most effective way to avoid being caught in learners' filters is to incorporate into the workshop design teaching methods that take into account sensory-intake levels and that appeal to various learners.

FIGURE 12-1   Sources of sensory information

What percentage of all sensory information we receive comes through each of the five senses?

Taste	_____
Hearing	_____
Sight	_____
Touch	_____
Smell	_____
TOTAL	100%

Source: Harold D. Stolovitch and Erica J. Keeps called *Telling Ain't Training* (ASTD, 2002).

Answers, top to bottom: 1.0%, 11.0%, 83.0%, 1.5%, 3.5%

Information Retention

Once information gets through the filter, it gets dumped into short-term memory. How short is short-term memory? Think about the last time you were introduced to someone at a party, and within seconds their name had disappeared from your memory. Short-term memory can be extremely short and extremely limited. Although you might be able to remember one person's name after an introduction, how many people can you meet before you are overloaded and can't remember anyone's name at all?

Information overload is the learner's enemy. It's the saturation point for short-term memory. There is no more room left for one more piece of information. Beyond that point, any more information starts to leak out. The instructor becomes irrelevant and nothing more can be learned by the learner.

Designers and instructors, therefore, need to deliberately design content to avoid information overload.

Reducing Information Overload

The rule of thumb in the training industry for the amount of information that can sit in a person's short-term memory is "7, plus or minus 2." In other words, generally speaking, people can take in an average of seven pieces of information at a time, but depending on the person and the situation that number could be as low as five or as high as nine.

What does one piece of information mean? That depends on what the learner knows already and how the information is presented. As an example, look at teaching Boolean operators to beginners. Saying that there are three Boolean operators, And, Or, and Not, would equal three pieces of information. Saying or demonstrating that "If you need to combine two or more terms together in a search, you would use 'And,'" might be another piece of information. By the time all three operators have been explained, the instructor would have used up an allotment of six pieces of information. This would be fine, because the allowable range is 7, plus or minus 2.

However, what if the instructor was able to combine some of the information pieces? Teaching the rhyme "Or is more, And is less," could be considered one chunk of information because learners can take that in together. A more common example of this is area codes. For those living in the Twin Cities area, 612 is one chunk. It means the area code for Minneapolis. For someone living elsewhere, this number would most likely be taken in as three separate pieces of information, 6 and 1 and 2.

Remember learning the multiplication tables for nine on your hands? This trick made all the nines-times tables into one informational item. Remember learning how to play an instrument and being taught "Every good boy deserves fudge?" Each of the first letters of this phrase relates to the order of notes on a staff. This trick makes the five notes into one informational item. This would allow between four to six more informational items to slip into the short-term memory.

It also helps that the more advanced the learner, the less information that might be considered a separate thing to learn. Let's say that you're designing a training session for catalogers and want to teach how to use the most common subfields in the main entry field of the MARC record. To a beginner cataloger, the five common subfields would be taken in as five separate pieces of information. But for catalogers who already have these subfields tucked into their long-term memory, they might be considered one piece of information called "Main Entry Subfields." If there was some way to group the subfields for the beginners into a word or a sentence that would help them memorize this list, then those five subfields could be construed as one informational item for this learner group as well.

Moving Information into Long-Term Memory

Think of the short-term memory as a small compartment in our heads. When the compartment is full but more information keeps coming in, the old information starts to leak out. There simply isn't any more capacity to store information. Many of us have experienced this phenomenon. We "just" learned something five or ten minutes ago, but it has seemingly slipped out of our heads and it's as if we never learned it at all.

The better alternative is to have current information move from short-term to long-term memory so that new information can be comfortably held in short-term memory. The challenge for designers and instructors is to get as much information into long-term memory as possible so that the short-term memory is free for more learning.

The main way designers and instructors can facilitate this movement from short-term to long-term memory is by getting the learner to apply what he or she has learned. In short, this means the learner has to do something with the information. The act of doing something with the information helps to move that information out of short-term memory and free up more space. The formula then is to cover 7 points (plus or minus 2) and then have the learner do something with those points. Then cover another 7 points, and have the learner do something with those points, and so on.

So, in simple terms, a workshop formula might look like this:

✔ ✔ ✔ ✔ ✔ ✔ ✔ (about 7 pieces of information)
   Learners say, write, do something

✔ ✔ ✔ ✔ ✔ ✔ ✔ (next 7 pieces of information)
   Learners say, write, do something

✔ ✔ ✔ ✔ ✔ ✔ ✔ (next 7 pieces of information)
   Learners say, write, do something

At the end of the workshop learners say, write, do something that relates to the entire workshop.

Try It Out

Edgar Dale's Cone of Experience illustrates that the more active the "doing," the more effective it is in increasing retention. The Cone of Experience (figure 12-2) shows that saying, writing, and doing things help the learner retain information. In other words, the act of saying, writing, and doing things helps to dump out the short-term memory and move that content to their long-term memory.

> ## Tip
>
> "What I hear, I forget; what I see, I remember; what I do, I understand." —Confucius

PAF Model

The PAF Model (figure 12-3) more thoroughly illustrates this simple concept. The model breaks down instruction into three phases—presentation, application, and feedback. The presentation (or P) phase relates to the check marks in the basic workshop formula above. The application (or A) phase relates to the "say, write, and do something" part of the formula. What is added is the feedback (or F) phase, in which the instructor and the learners get and give feedback on the learning.

FIGURE 12-2 Edgar Dale's Cone of Experience

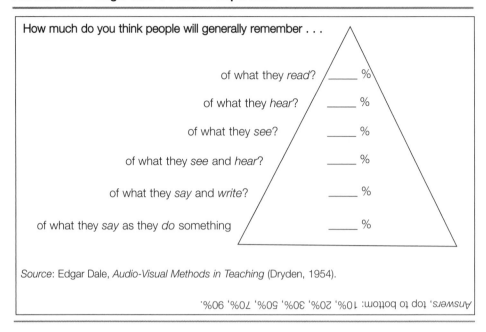

How much do you think people will generally remember . . .

of what they *read*? _____ %

of what they *hear*? _____ %

of what they *see*? _____ %

of what they *see* and *hear*? _____ %

of what they *say* and *write*? _____ %

of what they *say* as they *do* something _____ %

Source: Edgar Dale, *Audio-Visual Methods in Teaching* (Dryden, 1954).

Answers, top to bottom: 10%, 20%, 30%, 50%, 70%, 90%.

FIGURE 12-3 PAF Model

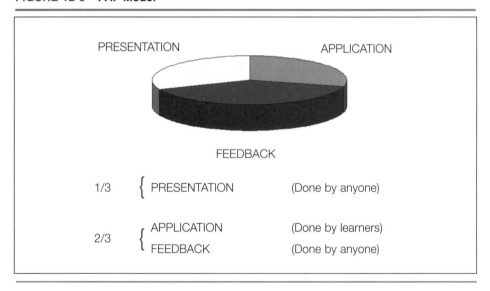

PRESENTATION   APPLICATION

FEEDBACK

1/3 { PRESENTATION   (Done by anyone)

2/3 { APPLICATION   (Done by learners)
     { FEEDBACK   (Done by anyone)

Presentation

In this model, only *one third* of the total time spent in a workshop should be spent presenting content. Presentation of content does not have to be taught in a lecture mode. Learners might read a handout, meet in pairs and then teach each other the content, or learn by doing and reflecting, for example.

Application

The rest of the workshop time should be spent on application and feedback. Application is the point at which the learners translate the content into a practical activity. Application is the only stage in the PAF Model that is done only by the learners. Watching the instructor conduct a demonstration is not an application.

As was mentioned in step 10, in a one-shot workshop the application and the check for understanding are often collapsed into the same activity in order to save time. Applications, just like checks for understanding, are controlled exercises in which the learners practice a skill or set of skills, or respond to written questions.

Often the application phase is when the light bulbs go off, when the click takes place. Learners who have been only partly following the instruction and others who have been drifting off or just nodding blankly are now called to task. The application phase is their learning opportunity to "really get it." Each learner is required to complete the assigned task. The instructor and assistant make sure each worksheet is filled out. The successful completion of this activity ensures the instructor that the objectives are being met throughout the workshop.

Feedback

Feedback can occur during or just after the application portion of the workshop. Feedback can be generated by the instructor, assistant, or by the learners. Feedback goes both ways. It is an opportunity for the instructor to get feedback on how well she is teaching, and for the learners to get feedback on their attempts to master the material. This is the time when the learner who is off track can be set straight, when the successful learner is praised, and when the instructor can clear up any confusion before moving on in the lesson. Feedback that occurs during the application portion of the lesson plan has the added benefit of allowing extra time during this stage in the process.

> **Tip**
>
> Most of the class content is learned during the application portion of the workshop—and not when the instructor is lecturing or demonstrating. Many learners who would normally fall through the cracks are reached during this time.

Timing

The time distribution of the PAF Model can be an enormous challenge, given that only one third of the total workshop time should be devoted to presenting information. Instead, the bulk of the time needs to be spent in helping the learners process this information and move it from their short-term memory to their long-term memory. In others words, if the instructor is doing all the work in the workshop, the learners are probably not learning much. Their short-term memory is getting overloaded, with no opportunity for them to free up more space. Therefore, the more application and feedback that is occurring in the classroom, the more short-term memory space is being freed up for more information.

It follows that if presentation is limited to "7 plus or minus 2" items, then application (the "say, write, do" part) and feedback will take place frequently during a workshop. Application and feedback cannot be saved for the very end of the workshop. Each module of the workshop may therefore consist of at least one round of presentation, application, and feedback, but some may have several rounds.

Kolb's Adult Learning Cycle

The learning cycle developed by David Kolb supports the PAF Model. Kolb's research helps instructional designers balance teaching techniques so that all learners—regardless of learning style—can learn most effectively. Kolb is best known for his identification of learning style types. From this work he created an Adult Learning Cycle that is used to show how learning should be presented in a way that is inclusive of each major learning style. (See figure 12-4.) This gives learners a well-rounded approach that includes aspects of each of their preferred learning styles. Use of the Adult Learning Cycle greatly increases the likelihood that the instructor is able to reach *every* learner for at least a segment of the workshop.

Kolb's learning cycle shows that the best learning includes four components: the ability to learn by observing and discussing, the ability to learn by hearing and reading and thinking, the ability to learn by planning and doing, and the ability to learn just by doing. You may be able to remember the names of each part of the cycle by using this acronym:

FIGURE 12-4 Kolb's Adult Learning Cycle

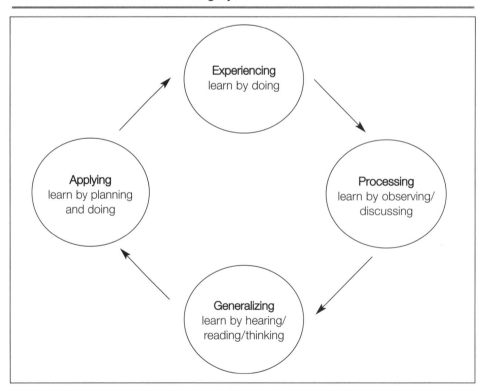

Processing

Applying

Generalizing

Experiencing

Including all four of these components in a workshop will provide every student with at least a portion of the workshop suited to their learning style. The next section of this chapter will describe how to do this.

TEACHING METHODS

Let's review what has been discussed in this chapter so far. In order to build on the understanding that human beings are filtering machines, instructors have to work to get their information through these filters. Short-term memory is so short that by the time you finish this sentence, you may have forgotten the preceding one. Short-term memory is so limited that it can only take in five to nine pieces of information at a time. Consequently, instructors have to build in application activities to free up short-term memory space so it can receive more information. The PAF Model has to occur frequently throughout the workshop, and teaching techniques should be designed to work with a variety of learning styles The designer needs to be able to draw on a wide-ranging toolkit of teaching methods.

Try It Out

What are some methods that you currently use in your teaching? Lecture and demonstration would appear on almost everyone's list. What else? Do you give students exercises to complete? Do you have open lab time when students work on their own projects? Do you give students search guides to read and then work from in class? Most librarians may find they already have a fairly good variety of teaching methods to choose from. But for designers working solo, it might be helpful to sit down with a colleague to help stimulate their thinking.

Teaching Methods Toolkit

It is important now, when selecting teaching methods, to keep two things in mind:

Teaching methods should map to either the presentation or the application phase of instruction.

The methods should reflect all aspects of the Adult Learning Cycle (processing, applying, generalizing, experiencing).

The designer is only limited by his or her imagination. To start the process, the designer should work with one module at a time.

Teaching Method Ideas

There are many creative teaching methods. Those listed below (adapted from Langevin Learning Services) are grouped according to whether or not the method relates to presentation, application, or in some cases to both presentation and application. Adapt these, use them to stimulate creative ideas, or just pick a few to start with. Remember, just using even one or two methods per workshop can make the session more effective than not.

Presentation Methods

The following are teaching methods that would be used to deliver the workshop content. These fall under the "presentation" type in the PAF Model.

Colloquy

> Create teams of three to five people. Identify areas of expertise for each team and assign readings or tasks for the "experts" to master. Then the learners ask questions, raise issues, and make comments for the experts to respond to. This method works well with the "Reading" technique below.

Conference

> Make available a number of different presentations for the learners to choose from. Generally the people at each session share a common problem, need, or interest.

Debate

> Assign an issue and have two learners or teams of learners defend opposite sides of this issue. Learners alternate in presenting their arguments. The purpose is to explore all aspects of an issue and also emphasizes winning.

Demonstration

> Demonstrate the performance of a task or procedure for learners to observe. The demonstration may be live or prerecorded using screen cam movies (such as from Camtasia Studio).

Dialogue

> Identify resource people or selected learners to hold a conversation while the learners observe. They may either present opposing views or simply discuss the issue in an informed manner.

Discussion

> Moderate an exchange of ideas on a topic of mutual concern. It can be totally unstructured and spontaneous or it can be highly structured.

Expanded Panel

> See "Panel" below. For this variation, create a panel group with a vacant chair. Learners can temporarily take the vacant chair in order to participate briefly in the panel discussion. When they have said what they need to say, they leave the chair so that others can take a turn.

Field Trip

Take learners to the place where the task is actually performed. Make sure the trip is not just another tour by planning the trip carefully for learning through observation and analysis of what is observed.

Instruments

Administer questionnaires, checklists, worksheets, or surveys that help learners gain insight about themselves or explore a topic.

Interview

Provide a resource person for learners to interview. Alternatively, have someone else conduct the interview and have the learners observe.

Jigsaw

Learners are put in small groups and assigned a reading to digest. Each group then teaches what they have learned to the whole class. The instructor guides and clarifies the group presentations as necessary.

Job Aids

Create worksheets, checklists, samples, flowcharts, procedural guides, glossaries, diagrams, decision tables, or manuals that will help learners complete a task either in the workshop or at their home/office/school.

Lecture

Deliver an oral presentation.

Lecturette

Deliver a very brief oral presentation. Can be only a few minutes or up to six or seven minutes. These might be interspersed throughout a workshop.

Listening Teams

Divide the workshop participants into teams. Assign each team an aspect of a topic. Then have the teams listen to a speaker or your lecture and take notes on their assigned aspect of the topic. In their groups they are then asked to prepare questions, summarize the relevant information, and then report their observations and conclusions to the entire workshop.

Panel

Create a panel of experts who hold a discussion while learners observe and ask questions. A moderator is helpful at directing the flow and making sure topics are on target.

Question and Answer

Cover the workshop content by asking a series of questions. You can also reverse this technique so that learners generate and ask questions in order to learn about the topic.

Reaction Team

A team of two to five learners is selected to react to a speaker's presentation by asking questions or making comments. They may be allowed to interrupt to seek immediate clarification.

Reading

In order to cover content or prepare for a group session, assign learners to read predetermined materials.

Reflection

Give learners time alone to review, think about, and jot down what has been learned and how it might apply given their situation.

Seminar

This is a participatory method in which learners are expected to have a good background in the topic and work together as equals. It may start with a brief presentation, after which the instructor becomes a resource person and learners are responsible for directing their own efforts. This method is commonly used in graduate programs.

Skit

Students prepare and rehearse a short dramatic presentation to illustrate principles or provide material for analysis and discussion.

Slip Writing

Quickly generate a list of questions from learners by asking everyone to write their main question on paper and pass it to the instructor. The instructor reads all the questions to the group and either answers or refers questions back to the group. This method can be used at any time a learner wishes to ask a question anonymously.

Study Guide

Create a study guide that will serve as a map for learners to follow as they are learning the subject. The guide can include many types of activities and materials and be used individually or in groups.

Think-Pair-Share

This is a quick method to create participation and stimulate thinking. Learners are given an issue or question, or are asked to generate questions to ask and are given several minutes to think and jot down some thoughts. Then they are paired up with another learner and asked to speak with them about the issue or questions. Each pair designates a speaker and key points from the discussion are shared with the rest of the learners. This method is also known as "Neighbor Discussions."

Video

Show a video. Tell learners what to look for in it so that the follow-up application will be more useful.

Application Methods

This next list is of teaching methods that would be used to facilitate the hands-on portion of the workshop. These fall under the "application" type in the PAF Model.

Action Learning

Learners work on solving an actual problem they might encounter in the real world. They analyze the problem and develop a plan to address it. When possible, they also implement the solution and study the effects of the implementation.

Clinic

Learners meet to analyze and "treat" a specific problem or react to a problem they have encountered.

Critical Incident

This is a variation of the case study in which the instructor gives learners incomplete information. By analyzing the case and asking the right questions, learners gain the additional information needed to solve the case.

Critique

Have learners analyze the strengths and weaknesses of a process, approach, system, or proposal and make suggestions for improvements.

Drill

Create a session with repetitive practice designed to increase efficiency in a task, improve the quality of performance, or aid in retention.

Game

Design a game in which competition or cooperation or both are used to practice skills or teaching points learned previously. Give out small prizes or treats if possible to the winners.

In-Basket

Give prepared items to the learners as if arriving in their in-baskets. Learners must place the items in priority order, make decisions, handle any difficulties, and respond to time deadlines and pressure in order to get the work completed.

Laboratory

Set up a site that allows for experimentation and testing by learners. Provide guidance and feedback.

Mini-Case

This is a slight modification of the case study. Describe a brief situation, using only key facts. Have learners discuss how the case should be handled. This method is often used to give examples of situations and procedures.

Practice Exercise

Give learners a specific and well-structured assignment that has them practice performing a task.

Quiz

Create and administer a questionnaire or test as a way of giving learners practice and of giving instructors a method of assessing learning.

Role Play

Create scenarios and have learners enact the situation in order to try out new skills or apply what has been learned.

Simulation

Set up the training space to allow learners to practice a task under very realistic conditions. Create a situational simulation. *Simulation* is often used as a blanket term for any realistic type of exercise. Role playing and case studies can be categorized as simulations.

Syndicates

Subdivide students into small teams of three to six people to perform an assigned task as a team.

Presentation and Application Methods

Presentation and application methods can be applied simultaneously using the following methods.

Behavior Modeling

Demonstrate "desirable behavior" and then have the learners analyze that behavior. Next create an opportunity for learners to practice the behavior with guidance and feedback.

Brainstorming

Assist learners in generating ideas. First facilitate the brainstorming of creative ideas without any criticism or judgment. Next have learners analyze and evaluate the ideas.

Committee

Create small teams of learners to work on different projects or assignments. Have each team report back to the larger group for direction and feedback.

Computer-Based Training

Assign students to a tutorial module for instruction and activities and for feedback via interaction with the tutorial.

Fishbowl

This is similar to the "Discussion" method. Divide the learners into two groups. The inner circle discusses an issue or does an exercise, while the outer circle observes and then offers observations or feedback. Then switch groups.

Learner-Controlled Instruction

Provide learners with all the resources they need in order to identify learning objectives, select resources, set up a program of study, and work through the program of study. Provide guidance.

Peer-Assisted Learning

Have learners help each other and provide feedback while completing an exercise under the instructor's guidance. This method can be used to give advanced learners an opportunity to help their peers.

Programmed Instruction

This is a self-instruction method in which trainees work through materials at their own pace, making responses and receiving feedback on their work. It can be done in many formats and media.

Self-Directed Learning

Learners create their own learning objectives, find learning resources, implement their learning objectives, and identify their own learning outcomes.

Brainstorm!

Now is the time to take these methods, what the design team knows about the learners and how people learn in general, and think creatively about how to deliver the workshop content. During the brainstorming stage, generate as many approaches to teaching the content as you can. This is the time to break out of the lecture–demo–hands-on formula! Admittedly, for some this might be one of the more challenging parts of the design process. Do you remember the brainstorming process from step 3?

1. Form your brainstorming group (if possible).
2. Identify the module of the workshop you will work on first. Review the task analysis, objectives and teaching points.
3. Brainstorm following the process described in step 3.

Some Ideas to Stimulate Brainstorming

In preparation for the brainstorming session, the following are some ideas to stimulate your thinking:

Talk to some innovative primary, secondary, and college teachers to get ideas flowing.

Ask your family to talk about their peak learning experiences and figure out what teaching methods were used.

Throw around some really fun, different kinds of ideas with some risk-taking colleagues.

If working in a team, set aside several blocks of time for more formal brainstorming. For a description of the brainstorming process, see step 3.

Let the ideas in the list of teaching methods above stimulate further ideas. Try taking several methods and fitting them together, or dropping some aspects and adapting others. Just remember to include both presentation and application methods and to work in opportunities for feedback.

Pull in some really creative people for this step.

Let the imagination run wild.

Use the library literature. There are many excellent books that offer creative teaching methods geared toward libraries. Some of these books are:

Trudi Jacobson and Timothy H. Gatti, *Teaching Information Literacy Concepts: Activities and Frameworks from the Field* (Library Instruction Publications, 2001)

Marilyn P. Whitmore and Sarah Brick Archer, *Empowering Students: Hands-on Library Instruction Activities* (Library Instruction Publications, 1996)

Gail Gradowski, Loanne Snavely, and Paula Dempsey, *Designs for Active Learning: A Sourcebook of Classroom Strategies for Information Education* (American Library Association, 1998).

Joanna M. Burkhardt, Mary C. MacDonald, and Andre J. Rathemacher, *Teaching Information Literacy: 35 Practical, Standards-Based Exercises for College Students* (American Library Association, 2003).

SUMMARY

Humans are amazing filtering machines. Don't get caught in these filters. Information overload can sink a workshop. Facilitate the movement of content from short-term memory to long-term memory by giving learners a chance to frequently apply their learning during the workshop. Use the PAF Model to guide the distribution of time spent on presentation, application, and feedback.

It is also critical to keep in mind that learners often represent the full gamut of learning styles. Some learners need to observe and discuss, but others need to learn by doing and applying. Incorporate a mix of teaching methods that reach as many of the learning styles of the targeted learners as possible.

Case Study

In the Unravel workshop series, the designers are encouraged to take risks during this stage and suggest new and different teaching methods. The level of creativity depends on who is in the room. Some designers are not as comfortable with this more creative side of the design process, while others come alive and get excited.

An early "experiment" in teaching methods was thought up by one of our most creative design team members. We were working on a module of a workshop that dealt with the library catalog and covered what a catalog was and what one could find in our catalog. Our challenge was to find a mental model that the learners currently had and that we could apply to a catalog.

We could have a short PowerPoint presentation on "what a catalog is and what's in it." We could ask the students to guess what it was and what was in it. We could give them some readings and then ask them to come up with the answer. We could have a quiz game where they guess and win prizes. We could give students a bunch of catalog records and ask them to figure out the answers using these. The ideas went on and on until finally someone said, "What about comparing mail-order catalogs with the library catalog?" Mail-order catalogs have particular kinds of items (you can't find computers in the J. Crew catalog, for example). They also have only certain descriptive information (such as size and color) and don't actually have the particular item available in it. You have to order it or go into the store to get it. Now that sounded good!

The design team took a break and came back the next week to look over the brainstorm list again. Some in the group were a bit leery of the catalog idea, but all agreed it would certainly be different, might be effective, and was worth a try in the pilot of the workshop. Eventually we designed a little lesson and exercise (presentation, application and feedback) around this teaching method that involved bringing in piles of our catalogs for students to use during the class. You'll find out what happened with this approach in subsequent chapters.

Are You All Set?

Have you

- ✔ Thought about the various ways that people learn and retain information?
- ✔ Taken an inventory of your current teaching methods and mapped them to the PAF Model?
- ✔ Talked to others to help stimulate creativity and help you think of additional teaching methods you might try?
- ✔ Put at least some items on the list that would take you out of your comfort zone?

STEP 13

Choose Teaching Methods

Once the instructional designer has brainstormed a list of possible teaching methods, the next step is to evaluate these ideas, choose the best methods, and then fine-tune them.

PROCESS FOR CHOOSING TEACHING METHODS

One way to help the designer evaluate the brainstormed list is to weigh each method idea against the following factors:

> *Time*—Can the method realistically fit into the allotted time?
>
> *Space*—Is there enough room to do this? Will you have the right equipment and setup?
>
> *Cost*—Does the method involve supplies, props, or incentives that must be purchased or rented?
>
> *Instructor confidence*—Does the instructor believe he or she can implement the method well? How confident is the designer in the instructor's abilities?
>
> *Level*—Is the method geared to the appropriate level for the particular learner group? Is it too sophomoric, too advanced, too chaotic, or too highly structured?

Once an initial elimination takes place using these factors, sort the remaining methods into presentation, application, and both presentation and application categories. Assess how the methods might fit together if they were used in the same module or the same workshop. Are there too many presentation methods and not enough application methods or vice versa? What kind of variety of methods is there? Are there methods that include processing, applying, generalizing, and experiencing as in Kolb's learning cycle? Use this information to eliminate teaching methods or further refine the remaining ones.

Then, finally, if some clear winners have not yet emerged, set aside some ideas for other modules in the workshop or for future workshops and settle on something to test in the pilot workshop.

> *In the first version of Unravel 1, there was a lot of lecture and the students were nodding off. The next semester we added in an extra activity that meant they had to do the very thing that I was talking about. The thing was, they couldn't do it. It was such a rude awakening to know that no matter how nice you were up there talking, they weren't necessarily going to take it in.*
>
> —Lynne Beck, Library Assistant, Government Publications Library, University of Minnesota Libraries–Twin Cities

FINE-TUNING THE TEACHING METHODS

What might be left on the brainstormed page is a broad idea of a teaching method. For example, in a workshop on avoiding plagiarism, a designer might want to do this: "Have two teams of learners debate the issue of the faculty using turnitin.com to reduce plagiarism. Teams alternate in presenting their arguments. The judge declares a winning team and gives out prizes (library-approved candy?) to the winners."

Next, the designer would picture this part of the workshop and begin to fill in the details. What exactly happens when the teams are formed? Do they work together to build a list of arguments? Do all learners have to speak, or just a designated learner? Do they each get a flipchart to capture their argument? Is there a worksheet they fill out? Do they get any questions prompting them in developing their argument? Do they need a fact sheet or an article to help them as well? Are they asked to present their argument ahead of time as an assignment from the client and then come to the workshop prepared to debate? How and when will the learners and the instructor give and receive feedback?

The intention of this part of the step is to begin applying the teaching method to the actual material. If it turns out that the method does not seem to work particularly well for this material or seems too complicated or time-consuming, choose another on the list.

SUMMARY

A number of factors contribute to the narrowing of the brainstormed list of teaching methods, including time, space, cost, instructor confidence, and the appropriateness of the method for the target learner group. After choosing the final teaching methods, the designer expands the method from an abstract one (e.g., "jigsaw application") into a practical one (e.g., break into groups, read one of the three articles on Google Scholar assigned to your group, identify five key points, and have each group member report on one key point to the class). These logistical details will help the designer in the next step in the design process: structuring the workshop.

Case Study

Like any group of people, the Unravel design team was made up of staff that had many different preferred styles of learning. Some learned best by listening and watching and argued for teaching methods suited to that style, while others wanted learners to jump headlong into a task and then find out what they didn't know and get help. Some wanted a hybrid of these approaches. In addition, those of us on the design team who taught frequently were also more apt to want to support methods similar to what we were currently using. The idea of possibly losing control of a class in order to have frequent applications made a few people clearly nervous. Too many had experienced students asleep in the back row, or checking their e-mail or ESPN, and who wanted to risk that again?

Choosing methods as a team was therefore a process of compromise. In a sense, everyone on the design team got a chunk that worked well for them. We encouraged team teaching so that the more experimental approaches might be covered by an instructor up to the challenge, while the more traditional approaches were covered by the instructor in a better position to take those on.

What methods were used? In the module on distinguishing between popular and scholarly citations discussed in step 9, the team chose methods that included reading (presentation), a worksheet done in pairs (application), and a voting process with structured feedback (feedback).

In a module on searching for known items in the library catalog, the team originally designed the module to begin immediately with the distribution of a bibliography and a one-minute demonstration (presentation) on how to get into the online catalog. Learners were then asked to find a mix of books and articles on the bibliography (application). The instructor and assistant assisted each student during this hands-on period (feedback). Then the instructor highlighted the three "pitfalls" that caused most of the problems for the students (presentation): you cannot use the words *the*, *a*, or *an* at the beginning of the title; use "TC" (which stands for "Twin Cities") to identify our campus libraries; and most important, you need to search the catalog for the name of the magazine, journal, or newspaper rather than the article title because articles are not listed in the catalog.

Notice how neither of these modules has a formal lecture. Our goal was to make sure that learners could apply the learning and make behavioral changes. Taking time for lectures would have gotten in the way of this.

Are You All Set?

Have you

- ✔ Evaluated your ideas?
- ✔ Chosen the best teaching methods for your purposes?
- ✔ Conducted a mental walk-through of each module and outlined the practical details of the method?

Structure Workshop

Finally the designer is at the point where the many disparate parts of the workshop are tied together into a lesson plan. How detailed this lesson plan is will depend on several factors:

> Will others besides the designer be using it to teach the workshop?
>
> If not, what is the likelihood that other library instructors may want to "borrow" some or all of the workshop?
>
> Will the lesson plan be part of a teaching portfolio used for staff performance evaluations?
>
> Will the lesson plan be shared with the client or with any potential clients?
>
> Will modules of the lesson plan ever be packaged so clients can teach parts of the workshop themselves?
>
> Will it be imperative that the instructor complete the lesson plan in the time allotted?
>
> Will the instructor need to adhere to careful timing for each module and for each segment within each module?

If the answer to any of these questions is yes, it might be helpful to develop a comprehensive lesson plan that fully scripts the workshop from beginning to end.

Anyone who works at a public service desk knows that there are probably a thousand ways to describe concepts or instruct on how to do research. By having a standard lesson plan and handouts for our library instruction classes, we are able to achieve two important outcomes: many more staff are able—and willing—to teach our students, and students receive consistent instruction in concepts, skills, and best practices.

—Julia Kiple, Stack Services, University of Minnesota Libraries–Twin Cities

This would include precise wording and transitions between segments and the major workshop modules. It would also include the background information that informed the designer's decisions (such as objectives, need-to-know list) and that would serve to justify decisions made in the lesson plan.

If none of the above questions are true, then the design team might come up with an outline lesson plan. This would allow some freedom to embellish and experiment with some slightly different approaches. You will see an example of this kind of lesson plan later in this chapter.

BUILDING THE COMPREHENSIVE LESSON PLAN

A comprehensive scripted lesson plan includes instructor's notes, an introduction, and each workshop module that has its own common elements.

The script starts with instructor's notes that address the logistics the instructor needs before starting the workshop. These may include:

- Goal(s) of the workshop
- Room setup
- Materials (such as handouts)

The workshop introduction is next. The introduction includes:

- A welcome to the learners
- The benefits of taking the workshop:

  Use your personal experience:

  > "When I was researching my last paper I had citations written out on scraps of paper, I had some in my e-mail account, I had a bunch of articles in a pile—it was a mess! When I got around to making my bibliography it took me hours! Now I just use RefWorks and it's saved a ton of time."

  Cite facts, statistics, or a reputable source to show the workshop's relevance:

  > "Last month an article in the *Wall Street Journal* showed that productivity decreases markedly when employees lack the skills to find and evaluate information they need to make informed decisions in the workplace."

  Demonstrate quickly:

  > "Yesterday I was working with a library user who was looking all over the Web for an article she needed. Within one minute I found it here, in a library database."

  Ask a question so that the learners tell you the benefit:

  > "Why do you think it is important to learn how to evaluate information?"

- Overview of the workshop:

    Tell how the workshop fits into the learners' larger goal (such as getting an A on a paper, getting a good job, or being more productive in their current job).

    Cover the workshop agenda (this should be a visual so learners can see where in the workshop they are throughout the session). Include how the workshop is going to be delivered (what the instructor will do, what the learners will do).

The introduction is followed by the first module. Each module of the lesson plan includes:

- That module's preparation for the instructor (for example, what they might need to write on a flipchart or white board)
- That module's objectives and teaching points for the instructor's background knowledge
- The script. This is what the instructor will say and is divided by presentation, application, and feedback segments.
- The estimated timing for each module. Within this estimate, time should be allocated for presentation, application, and feedback segments.
- Cheat sheets for the application (for example, instructor's guides to the worksheets that will be developed in step 15) worked into the lesson plan at the appropriate places
- A transition into the next workshop module

FORMATTING THE LESSON PLAN

There are many formats for lesson plans. Two kinds will be discussed here: an outline lesson plan and a highly scripted lesson plan. Use these formats and their levels of detail as departure points for creating a lesson plan script that you or your team are comfortable with.

Example of an Outline Lesson Plan

Figure 14-1 is an example of an outline lesson plan for a workshop module designed to teach learners how to go from a book or article citation they may have to finding the location of the actual book or journal in the library. The term "MNCAT" used within the figure is the name of the library's OPAC.

Example of a Comprehensive Lesson Plan

In contrast to the brief nature of the outline version of the lesson plan in figure 14-1, the scripted version shown on page 115 is much more detailed and tightly controlled.

This particular lesson plan is of a workshop called "Getting Started on Your Research" designed by the Minnesota Historical Society and taught to grades six through eight. The purpose of the workshop is to help students understand the basics of doing historical research in preparation for their visit to the History Center's library.

FIGURE 14-1   **Lesson plan for using the library catalog to find books and articles by citations**

Time	P/A/F	Content	Method	Resources
6 minutes	P	Introduction to this module First identify if looking for a book or article Go through PowerPoint: "Book or Article: You decide!" "An article citation has two titles: the title of the article and the title of the magazine or journal the article is in. A book citation has one title." "An article citation includes a volume, issue, and the month or exact date of the publication"	Lecturette	PowerPoint on desktop
2 minutes	A/F	Students complete worksheet Instructor roves and provides one-on-one feedback	Mutiple-choice worksheet	"Book or article: You decide!" worksheet
1 minute	F	Ask students for answers Reinforce correct answers Refer to teaching points above (in quotes)	Q&A	Using above worksheet
3 minutes	P	Demonstrate search for items from previous application Ask if the item is on the shelf Show holdings records, library location, and call numbers "Use 'TC' to identify our campus libraries"	Demo and Q&A	MNCAT and worksheet from above
15 minutes	A/F	Students complete bibliography on worksheet Instructor roves and provides one-to-one feed-back "MNCAT is the catalog of what the university libraries owns" "Need to search MNCAT for the name of the magazine, journal, or newspaper rather than the article title. Why? Articles are not listed in MNCAT."	Search catalog, complete worksheet	MNCAT access and worksheet
3 minutes	F	Summarize key challenges learners were having Reinforce "tips" on the worksheet	Lecturette	Worksheet

LESSON PLAN FOR "GETTING STARTED WITH YOUR RESEARCH"

Goals

Students will learn how to choose and narrow their research topic, including the importance of developing a thesis statement and locating primary sources to define their research. We want to give students tools to start thinking about how they can illustrate their thesis statement through arguments.

Grade Level

Grades 6 through 8 (adapt when necessary)

Setup

LCD (computer) projector

Northern Lights textbooks (created by the Education Department of the Minnesota Historical Society)

Five Harriet Bishop primary source boxes for application section on each table

Scratch paper and pencils on each table

Materials

The 5 "Ps" question criteria activity sheet (front for activity/back for their own project)

Extra pencils

Module 2 questions sheets for each box (each set deals with the primary source documents)

Harriet Bishop picture

5 "P" Question Board: this includes the 5 Ps and related questions, and the three thesis statements:

> During the mid-nineteenth century, Harriet Bishop communicated her middle-class, New England ideals to the people of St. Paul and created a new understanding of moral behavior that changed the community.

> In 1847 Harriet Bishop came to St. Paul as a teacher and communicated her ideals to her students.

> During the nineteenth century, many American women from the East communicated moral standards through their teaching in the West.

Mock call-number slips

Something to write on, such as a white board

Introduction

What have you decided for your topic for History Day? *Discuss topics.*

How is the research going? *Discuss research.*

So, you have picked your topic and started your research.

Let's say my topic is Altoids. I could tell you everything I know about Altoids—they were made in Great Britain, they have three calories each, and they give you curiously strong peppermint breath.

I could also look up everything I could find on Altoids from books, journals, magazines, and the Internet. But doing that would just be a report. I want to do more than just gather facts and present them. I want to take the facts and draw conclusions from them.

The conclusion that you make about your subject is a thesis statement.

You might think of it as saying, "So what?" So what that Altoids were made in England and they give you fresh breath. So what? The more you dive into research, the more you can answer the "so whats."

Today, I am going to help you answer those "so whats" and help you come up with a thesis statement.

Module 1: Answering the 5 P Questions (15 Minutes)

For Instructor:

OBJECTIVES

Given the 5 Ps and three examples of thesis statements, students will identify key components of a strong thesis statement.

TEACHING POINTS

A thesis statement is one or two sentences stating what you believe about your topic.

The 5 Ps are important parts of a strong thesis statement.

Presentation (5 minutes)

A thesis statement is one or two sentences stating what you believe about your topic. Let's take the example of Altoids again.

> Altoids is my topic.

(cont.)

Module 1: Answering the 5 P Questions (15 Minutes) *(cont.)*

A fact about Altoids is lots of teenagers eat them.
Yeah, so what?

Perhaps in doing a bit more research, I find that teenagers score much higher on IQ tests after they eat at least five Altoids. In doing even more research about intelligence and Altoids, I might conclude that not only do teenagers eat a lot of Altoids, but also that when teenagers eat Altoids, they become smarter. So my thesis statement might be something like:

Since the early 1990s, consumption of Altoids has caused a marked increase of intelligence in American teenagers.

And now some of you might be thinking, "Yeah, right. Like that could really happen. Prove it." And that is exactly what I have to do next! I have to prove my thesis statement.

And that is what you will be doing with your projects. After you have created a thesis statement, you will have to prove it by using at least three arguments. You need to take a stand, express a point of view!

On the top of this board, I have three thesis statements about a woman named Harriet Bishop who was the first public school teacher in St. Paul. One of these thesis statements is better than the others.

Just by reading them, let's take a vote on which thesis statement you think is the best. I'll read them first. *Tally votes.*

How can we figure out which thesis statement is just right? The 5 Ps might help. *Run through the five Ps (People, Period of Time, Purpose, Parallel to the Theme, and Proof).* In answering these 5 P questions, let's figure out which one is the best.

Application *(10 minutes)*

I will divide you into three teams: green, blue, and red.

Green group, this is your thesis statement. You will be answering questions for the green thesis statement only. I am also giving each one of you a sheet with the thesis statement and questions on it to record on your own. *Pass out sheets.*

Red group, this is your thesis statement. Again, red team, you will be answering questions for the red thesis statement. And here are your sheets. *Pass out sheets.*

And blue team, here is your thesis statement. You will be answering questions for the blue thesis statement. *Pass out sheets.*

Again, your main goal is to figure out which thesis is best out of the green, red, or blue thesis statements. By answering the 5 P questions, it will help you determine which thesis statement is the best.

Give students a few minutes to answer the first three questions of People, Period of Time, and Purpose. Discuss findings. Major points include:

PEOPLE: WHO WAS INVOLVED OR AFFECTED?

Green thesis: American women from the East

How many women would that be? (thousands)

Red thesis: Harriet Bishop and her students

How many people would that be? (eight)

Blue thesis: Harriet Bishop and the people of St. Paul

How many people would that be? (about 100)

PERIOD OF TIME: WHEN DID IT HAPPEN? WHAT WAS THE TIME PERIOD?

Green: Nineteenth century

How much time is in a century? 100 years is a long period of time to cover in your research and prove!

Red: 1847

Only one year. Will we be able to find enough evidence in our research?

Blue: Mid-nineteenth century

20–30 years

PURPOSE: WHY DID IT HAPPEN?
WHY SHOULD WE CARE?

Green: American women communicated their moral standards through teaching

Which American women?

What moral standards? Very broad

Red: Harriet Bishop communicated her ideals with her students

What ideals?

How did she communicate her ideals to her students?

Blue: She communicated her middle-class, New England ideals to the people of St. Paul and created a new understanding of moral behavior that changed the community

What moral standards or ideals?

(cont.)

Middle-class, New England ideals

   In communicating this to her students, what did she do?

   Created a new moral understanding that changed the community of St. Paul.

PARALLELS TO THE THEME

Link thesis to theme of the class assignment.

PROOF

And now for the last category, Proof. To answer this question, think about your answers to People, Period of Time, and Purpose. The answer to your question should also help in deciding which overall thesis is best. Here is the question. Can I reasonably try and prove this thesis statement? Is it too broad? Too narrow? Why or why not? *Discuss as a large group*.

   Also, ask students if they can really argue and prove the red thesis statement. If I read in all of my sources that Harriet Bishop communicated her moral ideals to her students, can I argue that statement? *Discuss that the red thesis statement is really just a fact and not a thesis statement at all. A thesis statement needs to be an opinion. Can give this example if need to: Michael Jordan is a basketball player. Is that a fact or an opinion? (Fact) Now what if I said Michael Jordan is the best basketball player in the whole world. Fact or opinion? (Opinion)*

Module 2: Beginning the Research: Primary and Secondary Sources (30 Minutes)

For Instructor:

OBJECTIVES

Given actual primary source materials, students will be able to distinguish primary sources from secondary sources.

Given primary source materials about Harriet Bishop, students will apply the contents of primary sources to a research project on Harriet Bishop.

TEACHING POINTS

A primary source is information created by the event, in the process of the event, or by an eyewitness to the event in question.

Presentation (*10 minutes*)

Once you have decided on a topic, what are the best places to start researching? *Discuss Web, encyclopedia, textbook, etc.* To get an overview of your topic, these are great places to start. But then it is time to dive in deeper. Have you ever heard of the terms *primary and secondary sources? Discuss*.

PRIMARY SOURCES

A primary source is information created by the event, in the process of the event, or by an eyewitness to the event in question. Let's say we were studying student life from [their school] in 2005. Are you a primary source? What kinds of sources might be available? *Discuss (a picture of them, their clothing, shoes, jewelry, e-mails, diaries, report cards, etc., would all be primary sources). Highlight the various primary source examples from the list as necessary*.

   Besides primary sources, there's another kind of source that can help you find information about your project. *Discuss secondary sources*. How many of you have played the game "telephone"? What sometimes happens? You can think of a secondary source as playing telephone. The person who is saying something for the first time is the primary source, but it becomes a secondary source with the next person saying it. Most history books and textbooks are secondary sources. Successful research projects will use both primary and secondary sources.

Application and Feedback (*20 minutes*)

We have pulled out some primary sources about our topic of Harriet Bishop. Let's examine these primary sources to see what they tell us about Harriet Bishop. At each table you will find a box with primary sources and artifacts. *Discuss the use of white gloves for the very old and fragile materials*. Please examine the primary sources in the box and answer the three questions on your answer sheet. *Model and pass out boxes to tables. Work briefly with each group to help them understand and interpret their source. Go from table to table, having each group answer their question out loud. Have each group present their findings to the rest of the class*.

[*Note*: Module 3 is omitted. This is a virtual tour of the library in which students find call numbers and create mock slips for requesting library resources.]

SUMMARY

Lesson plans include notes to help the instructor understand the purpose of the workshop and the preparation needed, a compelling introduction, and clear directions to the instructor for each module of the workshop. Lesson plans can vary from outlines to full scripts.

Case Study

The Unravel design team intended our lesson plans to be used by instructional staff who were not part of the design team, and to be read by faculty who were not familiar with the subject content. We also wanted subject liaison librarians who weren't involved in the design to be able to take a module or two and adapt it to their higher-level workshops. These factors argued for the use of a fully scripted lesson plan.

An even more compelling argument for having a well-written and fully scripted lesson plan was that the team knew the allotted workshop time would be very tight. It would be imperative that the instructor not deviate too much from the script, since embellishments lead not only to information overload, but can add many minutes to each workshop module.

Because of this, it was tempting for some to cut off the end of the workshop and end before the last module. The objection to this was that every version of the workshop needed to reach the end of the script in the allotted time, since students from the same course would be coming to many different offerings of the workshop. Cutting out parts of the workshop because an instructor lost track of time might mean, for example, that some students would learn about popular and scholarly resources while other students from the same course module who attended a different Unravel workshop would not. Because of these reasons, the design team felt it needed to tightly script the lesson plan.

The exact formatting of the lesson plan is often customized by various instructors. The latest version of the lesson plan is located in Word on the Web (at http://staff.lib.umn.edu/rcs/usered/unravel.html) and allows instructors to change the formatting as they see fit.

EXAMPLE OF AN UNRAVEL WORKSHOP MODULE

The following module is a ten-minute segment in the "Unravel the Library 2: The Research Process" workshop.

MODULE 4: Scholarly vs. Popular (10 Minutes)

For Instructor:

PREPARATION

On white board, create the following chart:

	Scholarly	Popular	Don't know
1.			
2.			
3.			
4.			

On Unravel flipcharts (predesigned and available in the instruction room), locate the page that lists four criteria.

OBJECTIVE

Given a citation and abstract, use four criteria to distinguish between a scholarly citation and a popular citation.

TEACHING CONTENT

There are four key criteria for how to distinguish between scholarly and popular citations:

Vocabulary in citation: Is it conversational? academic?

Audience of journal or magazine: Is it written for a general audience? Academics/researchers?

(cont.)

Availability of journal or magazine: Can it be found on a newsstand? Academic only?

Length of article: Is it 1 or 2 pages? 15 or 20 pages?

Presentation and Application (*5 minutes*)

Read the handout called "Popular or Scholarly: You Decide." Then go ahead and fill out the worksheet.

Instructor and assistant: Please rove around the room, and provide assistance when necessary.

Presentation and Feedback (*5 minutes*)

Let's take a group vote and see what everyone thought. How many people said that the first citation is scholarly? *Record votes on board*. Popular? How many thought it might be part of the gray literature?

Scholarly	Popular	Gray
III	I	I

Why did those of you who said it was scholarly think that? *Use discussion points in box below so that the four criteria are emphasized for each item. Use the flipchart to emphasize the four criteria.*

1. *Journal of Applied Social Psychology*, May 2002 v32 i5 p1064 (19)

   Of tabloids and family secrets: the evolutionary psychology of gossip. Francis T. McAndrew; Megan A. Milenkovic.

   Two experiments tested hypotheses about gossip derived from an evolutionary perspective. The results of these experiments confirmed a consistent pattern of interest in gossip marked by a preference for information about others of the same age and gender. Exploitable information in the form of damaging, negative news about nonallies and positive news about allies was especially prized and likely to be passed on. The findings confirm that gossip can serve as a strategy of status enhancement and function in the interests of individuals, and that it does not just function as a means of social control within groups.

This is a scholarly journal article:

Length: This article is lengthy (19 pages). (The "Popular vs. Scholarly" guide describes "lengthy" as 5–50 pages.)

Vocabulary: The language used in the title and abstract is specialized and not very conversational.

Availability: The *Journal of Applied Social Psychology* is not widely available on newsstands.

Audience: The availability of the *Journal of Applied Social Psychology* and the language used in the title and abstract of this article suggest that it is intended for academics and researchers in the field.

Instructor: Follow the same formula above for the rest of the items.

2. *PC World*, Sept 1999 p 46 (2)

   Are Wired Schools Failing Our Kids? (technology literacy still an unfulfilled promise in most public schools) Roberta Furger.

   Although Pres. Clinton's Technology Literacy Challenge, passed in 1996, has greatly increased schools' Internet access overall, the poorer half of US school districts have untrained teachers and limited Internet access, as well as outdated software and computers. For permanent improvements, states should adopt long-term budgets and pass bond issues to hire technology staff capable of maintaining the new technology.

This is a popular magazine article:

Length: This article is short (2 pages). (The "Popular vs. Scholarly" guide describes "short" as 1–5 pages.)

Vocabulary: The language used is conventional, conversational, and easy for a general audience to understand.

Availability: *PC World* is available on local newsstands.

Audience: *PC World* is intended for a general audience.

3. *Literature-Film Quarterly*, Oct 2000 v28 i4 p312 (16)

   The deconstructive search for Oz (meaning in *The Wizard of Oz*) Steven Hamelman.

(cont.)

This article examines the critical interpretations of the classic film, *The Wizard of Oz*, focusing on the use of deconstruction in cultural criticism. Topics addressed include the portrayal of desire, good and evil, and home in the film.

This is a scholarly journal article:

Length: This article is lengthy (16 pages). (The "Popular vs. Scholarly" guide describes "lengthy" as 5–50 pages.)

Vocabulary: The language used in the title and abstract is somewhat specialized and not very conversational.

Availability: *Literature-Film Quarterly* is not widely available on newsstands.

Audience: The availability of *Literature-Film Quarterly* and language used in the title and abstract of this article suggest that it is intended for academics and researchers in the field.

4. *Discover*, March 2001 v22 i3 p31 (1)

From UFOs to IFOs. (unidentified flying objects; identified flying objects) Bob Berman.

The vast majority of unidentified flying objects can be identified by considering external factors, including reflection, astronomical phenomenon, and the number of artificial satellites in the sky. Factors to be considered are described.

This publication falls in a gray area (cannot be definitively defined as popular or scholarly). It could be described as a popular magazine article:

Length: This article is short (1 page). (The "Popular vs. Scholarly" guide describes "short" as 1–5 pages.)

Availability: *Discover* is available on local newsstands.

However, *Discover* also has some attributes of a scholarly journal:

Audience: *Discover* is intended for researchers in the sciences as well as for a general, nonacademic, nonspecialized audience.

Other: *Discover* contains sophisticated writing, footnoted articles, and authors that hold advanced degrees.

Gray area publications:

There are always gray areas with respect to pinning down what is popular or scholarly.

If you are concerned about whether an article you want to use falls within a particular category, talk with your instructor or reference librarian.

Are You All Set?

Have you

✔ Chosen whether to create a comprehensive lesson plan or a more abbreviated outline version?

✔ Created an introduction?

✔ Provided estimated times for each module and perhaps even for each segment within a module?

✔ Either created an outline or a detailed script for each module?

✔ Created transitions between each module?

Develop Materials

Back in the old days, remember how hard it was to use the manufacturer's directions to do things like put together a bed frame or a swing set? These directions were commonly written by the engineers who designed the product. In many cases it seemed like these engineers wrote for engineers—they used engineering-like terminology, assumed knowledge that many "ordinary" people did not have, and wrote dense text that made people anxious just looking at it.

Now, thankfully, there is an entire field devoted to the development of effective written materials. It's called "scientific and technical writing." The main association for this field, the Society for Technical Communication, has over 20,000 members who work in all kinds of industries. Technical writers are paid to write and design effective materials that consumers use every day. As those consumers, we can breathe a sigh of relief that companies have finally figured out that hiring technical writers pays off—not that written instructions are perfect now, but at least the consumer has a chance at programming that VCR or putting together that complicated swing set.

Obviously, most library staff are not trained in the field of technical writing, even though many of us do this work every day. Writing and designing pathfinders, other handouts, and web pages are often just "part of the job" of the regular librarian and staff. But try testing currently used written materials with some learners and it becomes fairly clear—it is challenging to write and design these kinds of materials. Learners will sometimes grimace at all the text, get confused by the language, and find it difficult to skim the material.

One tenet that we might follow is, "Do No Harm." In other words, the designer of the materials has to make sure they do everything they can *not to cause even more confusion* with the material covered in the workshop.

Beyond that, of course, the goal is to actually *increase the effectiveness* of the workshop through the inclusion of written materials. This chapter provides some tips and techniques to make high-quality written materials.

OVERVIEW

High-quality written materials can play an important role in increasing student learning. Visuals, handouts, and worksheets can

- Allow for teaching points to be heard and seen (the importance of both visual and auditory information was discussed in step 12)
- Provide an opportunity for visually oriented learners and note-takers to better keep up with the workshop
- Provide learners with "extra" material if applicable to the learner group. This material may cover some of the nice-to-know points that were dropped from the need-to-know list. It may also include all of a particular task analysis, even if some of the subtasks or steps were not covered in the workshop
- Give learners a task to complete which focuses their attention on the workshop content
- Reveal to the instructor what the learners do not fully comprehend or where their skills are still lacking

TYPES OF MATERIALS

There are four different types of materials that might be developed for a workshop. Most workshops will include some of all four types: visuals, handouts, worksheets, and hybrid materials.

Visuals

Visuals can either be projected or put on flipcharts or white boards. They may include graphic representations of content (such as a diagram or illustration), teaching points, and directions for application components. Visuals can be put on PowerPoint slides, transparency/acetate sheets, or flipcharts. They may also include photographs, drawings, maps, graphs, charts, and videos.

There are many ways to use visuals well. As they say, a picture is worth a thousand words, and diagrams, illustrations, or pictures can be used to illustrate key points. For example, a graphic of a scholarly journal cover and title can help learners understand just what a "journal" is, as they may never have seen one before. The name of the library catalog over a diagram of a circle with a line through it and the word "articles" inside may help some learners understand that articles are not found inside the library catalog. If the design team does not have any visually oriented members, pull in someone who can help think of visual ways to represent concepts or terms.

Another way to use a visual is to capture the teaching points for a particular module. At the start, in the middle, and at the end of each module the instructor might refer to these written or graphically represented teaching points. In this way learners not only hear the points but see them as well, which increases their retention.

Flipcharts

Before moving on, here are a few reasons to consider using flipcharts to show visuals instead of PowerPoint:

A flipchart easel can be placed on the side of the room, causing the instructor to move there to turn the pages. This pulls the attention of the learners from the papers in front of them, their desktops, and the screen in the front, which can jog some people to attention.

The lights can stay on with a flipchart.

A completed flipchart pad can be tucked in a corner and used over and over. It's easy to forget a disk or CD-ROM in an office, leave it in the classroom after the class, or even to "lose" a PowerPoint on the desktop.

If there are multiple instructors teaching the class, a flipchart can be used by even the most technically challenged among them.

Flipcharts can be filled in during the class. For example, the instructor may have a fill-in-the-blank sentence on the flipchart that he or she writes in during the class. As a side note, a common facilitator trick is to lightly pencil in "answers" or notes on the flipchart so that only they can see it. In this example, the fill-in-the-blank answer could be penciled so the answer is right there for the instructor.

Handouts

Learners may be directed to refer to the handouts during the workshop, or the handouts may be intended as supplementary information to be referred to later. Handout content could include

- The full task analysis (written in step 6)
- Teaching points (written in step 7)
- Copies of the visuals (written in this step)
- Space for note-taking

The volume and depth of the handouts should be learner-appropriate. For a group of novice learners, the handouts may be kept to a minimum and be blended with the worksheets, so that instruction is at the point-of-need in the application stage of the workshop. For more advanced audiences, on the other hand, this is where the designer might include some important nice-to-knows. Although these nice-to-know items are not covered in the workshop, the handouts would give learners additional information and reference materials for later use.

Worksheets

Worksheets provide learners with clear tasks to complete and the recognition that their work will be looked at, and even possibly graded. Whether or not this is actually true is not the point—just the *expectation* that it might be true can be a strong motivator for even the most uninterested learner to become engaged in a task.

Another strong motivation that worksheets provide is the fear of looking stupid. Because the instructor is paying attention during the application phase to what is being written on the worksheets, the learner who is not bothering to participate will end up getting extra attention. The instructor will ask what is confusing to the learner and help to relieve the confusion by working with that learner to complete the worksheet. Some learners will complete the worksheets just to avoid this extra tutoring.

More conscientious learners, on the other hand, may get a sense of satisfaction from the worksheets. The instructor can tell them that they're doing a good job; and if the worksheet includes optional advanced tasks or questions, the fast learner can move on to more challenging work.

Regardless of the learners' intrinsic motivation, worksheets prove to them that they actually learned something. The worksheets are assessment tools that, when looked over by the instructor, can tell learners if they "got it right" or not. And if not, the instructor can help them to finally get it and move on. This may give learners the confidence they need to continue to use the library for their research.

Worksheets may include

- Directions for applications and checks for understanding
- The task broken up with space to record their work
- Fill-in-the-blank, multiple-choice, or open-ended questions
- Hints or tips for doing well on the application or the check for understanding
- Optional or advanced tasks or questions
- Space for learners to record their work or answers

Hybrid Materials: Combining Handouts and Worksheets

Juggling several pieces of colored paper and trying to keep the right one in front of a learner is a hassle that can be avoided with hybrid materials. Combining handouts and worksheets into one packet may be an efficient way to keep learners on the correct page. Each packet can be stapled and each page numbered in sequence with the workshop delivery, so that the learner can easily move through the packet from beginning to end.

Interspersing information with activities in the same packet can also give learners the help they need for each worksheet activity where and when they need it.

The hybrid approach works particularly well when certain information not covered in an oral presentation segment is important for completion of the application; this information can be included on the hybrid materials before the application segment and learners asked to read this before beginning their application. This cuts back on lecture time and gives learners easy access to the content where and when they need to use it.

APPROACH TO MATERIALS

Aside from choosing the type of materials (visuals, handouts, worksheets, or a hybrid approach), there are still a few other issues to think about.

What tone should be used?

Formal? Informal? Professional? Conversational? Workshop materials can set a tone for the workshop. Do the format and tone of the workshop delivery match the format and tone of the written materials? Or do the materials need to reflect librarywide guidelines for publications that impact tone? Remember, the written materials may be taken away from the workshop, recopied, shared, and shown to the client. They will reflect on the library, the workshop, and the instructor.

What level of depth of information will the learners want or need?

Would they want to keep a step-by-step guide to completing all the tasks covered in the workshop? Would they want to have a copy of all the flipcharts or PowerPoints and teaching points? Would they just want your business card or a one-page list of resources and support for more help? Or would any of the preceding items most likely end up in the trash basket at the door of the classroom?

Should some materials be optional or should they all be required?

Printing can cost libraries a lot of money, and trees are valuable resources. Might some written materials be optional for those learners who are most interested?

WRITING MATERIALS

The following are some techniques to keep in mind when writing workshop materials.

KISS—Keep it short and simple.

>Remember the discussion of information overload? Don't let the handouts exacerbate this problem. Keep them short and simple, and include links to websites with more information if necessary.

Avoid jargon.

>For some learners a term as simple as *indexes* may be jargon. In this case, a definition of *indexes* might be set aside in a box as a reminder of what that word means.

Use active rather than passive verb forms.

>Passive verbs make a sentence more difficult to understand.

Use the Fog Index to measure the general readability of draft text.

>The Fog Index measures the approximate grade level for which the material is written. Try it by taking a 100-word sample from a library handout and averaging the number of words per sentence. Then count the number of words with three or more syllables (not including proper names and the three-syllable words in which the last syllable ends in ing, ed, or es). Add these two numbers. Then multiply this by 0.4. This number reflects the approximate grade level of the handout. To lower the grade level, try using more of the techniques just listed.

Test your materials on representative members of the learner groups. See the next module for information on conducting these tests.

Tip

For more information about the Fog Index, see Robert Gunning's book *The Technique of Clear Writing* (McGraw-Hill, 1971).

DESIGNING MATERIALS

Image isn't everything, but it is certainly important. What a written material looks like can affect whether learners bother to read it, how much of it they read, and whether they take it home with them, share it with others, and refer to it themselves later.

Some techniques that help include

White space

>Ironically, the amount of space *around* your text has an impact on whether or not the learner will read it. In fact, the use of white space can be the most important design element. Create white space by using gaps between lines and paragraphs, shorter paragraphs, wide side and top and bottom margins, indentation, and centering of text.

Headers

>Give learners a road map to the material by creating frequent headers. These should be specific, brief, and clear.

Signposts

>Write the first sentence of a paragraph or module so that learners can skim it and get a sense of the whole module.

Numbers and bullets

Use numbered or bulleted lists to help learners quickly make sense of the material. Do not go over four levels of subdivision.

Emphasis

Catch the learner's eye by emphasizing key words. Use bold, underlined, or capital letters, boxing, spacing, asterisks, a different font or color, or italics.

TESTING OUT MATERIALS

Once materials have been drafted, assume they are just that—a draft. Assume that these drafts will go through several rounds of revision. The first round can start within this step of the design process. Think of this process as a mini-usability test like the kinds that are used for website design projects.

1. Identify and Prep Volunteers

One of the easiest ways to test for clarity is to ask several student assistants or library volunteers to be part of your draft revisioning. If possible, work with just one or two volunteers at a time. Ask the test participants to put themselves in the shoes of the intended learner group and help uncover any possible areas of confusion they might have.

2. Get Initial Impressions

Show the volunteers the materials and ask them for their initial reactions on the layout and design. In other words, if they got this in a workshop, what would be their first impression? Do the layout and design make the written materials seem easy to read and follow? Are there any specific critiques about the layout? (Not enough white space? Too many fonts? Difficult to skim?) Are the visuals legible to learners even in the farthest seats?

3. Test for Effectiveness

Next, ask the volunteers to complete a task, follow a procedure, or answer a question that the materials cover. As they do this, ask them to think aloud. The test monitor should refrain from teaching, guiding, or doing anything to impact on the effectiveness of the materials.

If the material includes . . .	Then ask the volunteer test participant to . . .
a task analysis	complete the task using the handout only
teaching points	explain what they think the teaching point means using their own language
directions and an application	complete the worksheet
graphics	describe what they think the graphic means

4. Test for Textual Clarity and Vocabulary

Comments about textual clarity and vocabulary should have been made during the think-aloud portion of the preceding step. Now, however, is a chance to go over the whole handout, visual, or worksheet to make sure that all the vocabulary and text are clear to the volunteer. Are there any words that assume prior knowledge the learner might not actually have? Is every sentence clear?

If there are directions for completing a task, ask the volunteers to explain in their own words what they think the directions mean. If there are definitions, make sure they are convinced that each definition is easy to understand.

5. Make Changes

Making initial changes to the materials will make the pilot workshop go more smoothly and will reduce subsequent revisions down the road.

SUMMARY

Written and visual materials play an important role in a workshop design. They can include handouts, worksheets, flipcharts, transparencies, and PowerPoint presentations. Designing effective materials can be challenging. Make sure that they are tested with volunteer or representative learners and revised before implementation.

Case Study

The visuals for the Unravel 2 workshop include the following:

Flipcharts

Each instruction room has an identical set of completed flipcharts. They include a title page, an agenda, goals for the workshop, objectives for each module, and teaching points for each module.

PowerPoint

The only module of the workshop that has a PowerPoint is a lecturette that helps students identify whether or not a citation is a book or an article citation. The PowerPoint was chosen because it allows for animation to highlight the various components of the citation that indicate what type it is.

Hybrid packet of handouts and worksheets

The Unravel designers wanted to simplify the use of handouts and worksheets. By combining them into a stapled packet, students are easily able to follow along during the workshop.

Initially the hybrid packet reflected a mishmash of designs from the multiple authors who contributed to it. But eventually the packet was standardized with a common look and feel. Currently the Unravel 2 workshop packet includes the following:

Page one

A title page with the workshop goals and an "advertisement" for the Assignment Calculator, a tool that helps students fight procrastination (see http://www.lib.umn .edu/help/calculator/).

Page two

The title of the module ("Finding Articles") and bulleted teaching points set in a text box. Below this are step-by-step directions for completing the first application, which gives students a subject (the energy crisis), a topic based on the row they are in (e.g., how business views the energy crisis), and then has students choose three appropriate article indexes.

Page three

The title of the next module ("Finding Article Citations and Full Text") and bulleted teaching points set in a text box. Below this are step-by-step directions for completing the second application, which gives learners a topic (downloading music) and has them identify search terms, conduct the search, and review the results using open-ended questions.

Page four

The title of the module ("Using MNCAT to Find Books and Articles") and bulleted teaching points set in a text box. Next are the step-by-step directions for completing the application, "Book or Article? You Decide!" which has two citations and asks students to identify if the citation is a book or an article. The second question is multiple choice and asks them to answer which item in the catalog they would search with (title? author? etc.).

Page five

This is a continuation of the module covered on the previous page and so has the same title ("Using MNCAT to Find Books and Articles"). Below this are instructions for the next application, which has students search the catalog for the bibliography listed on this page of the packet. There are also three "tips" on this page that are not covered in the presentation, but which we ask students to read if they get stuck. The bibliography has seven items: some are journal articles, others are newspaper articles, and several are books. Next to each item is a box where students write the library the item is located in, and the call number for that item. Below the seven items is an "optional" item that is added for those who get through the bibliography faster than others. Answering this means that the learner has to find and implement an advanced search, a procedure that is not covered in Unravel 2.

Pages six and seven

This is a two-page handout on the characteristics of popular, scholarly, and gray materials.

Page eight

The title of the module ("Popular or Scholarly? You Decide") followed by step-by-step directions for completing the application. Four citations and abstracts are followed by a place for students to check which they think the citations are—popular, scholarly, or gray.

Page nine

This is the learning evaluation and is titled, "How Well Did We Teach You?" This includes eight multiple-choice questions.

Page ten

This is the second iteration of a reaction evaluation that we use for Unravel 2. This version asks four open-ended questions.

To see all of these materials, go to http://staff.lib.umn.edu/rcs/usered/unravel.html and look for the Unravel 2 worksheets from 2004–5.

Are You All Set?

Have you

✔ Identified the content needed for visuals?

✔ Chosen a format for each visual (e.g., PowerPoint, flipcharts, transparencies)?

✔ Identified the content needed for handouts?

✔ Listed the applications and checks for understanding that will need worksheets?

✔ Chosen the tone and depth of information for the written materials?

✔ Drafted the materials?

✔ Designed the visual elements of the materials carefully using white space, techniques for emphasis, signposts, bullets, and numbered lists?

✔ Gotten some initial feedback from volunteers who either represent the learner group or who are able to critique the materials from their perspective?

Pilot Workshop

You might think of each new workshop as an experiment in instructional design and delivery. Knowing that a workshop will be piloted before actual delivery gives the instructional designer some leeway to be bold and extra creative. This way, if there are glitches in the lesson plan, or if a certain application or presentation technique falls flat, there is still time to make adjustments.

TYPES OF PILOTING

There are several different approaches to choose from when it comes to pilot workshops.

External Pilot

For workshops that will be offered multiple times with outcomes "promised" to particular clients, plan for a full-fledged pilot. Locate representative volunteers from the learner group who agree to be your guinea-pig learners in the workshop. Teach the workshop as if they were an actual learner group, but then provide incentives for them to stay and discuss how the workshop went (this discussion will be covered later in this chapter).

Internal Pilot

If only one or two modules are being designed or if the final product can be less than perfect, it might be advisable (and easier) to pilot the modules or workshop with an internal group such as student assistants or library volunteers who need training in the area you are covering. Try to choose those who best reflect the target learner population, and run the workshop as if they were the actual learners. After the workshop is completed, facilitate a discussion on how it went.

Pseudo-Pilot

If running one of these types of pilots is not possible, think of the first offering of the workshop or module as a pilot. Just as you would in the previous types of pilots, provide incentives for learners to stay after the workshop for a debriefing on how the workshop went. Coffee and donuts, pizza, extra credit, or free coffee coupons might be enough to engage them.

COMPONENTS OF A PILOT

Instructor

This is the chance for the design team to take their design for a test drive. If the script is still in its early stages of development, consider having the lead designer be the instructor, since he or she might be in the best position to improvise and make up what's missing. If the designer is particularly bold and feels it would be helpful, videotape the pilot for later evaluation.

Observers

If the workshop is being designed by a team, as many members as possible should come to observe the pilot. If working as a solo designer, try to entice some trusted colleagues to be observers. Ask the observers to follow along with the script and note any problems such as inconsistent terminology, unclear explanations, and awkward content introductions or transitions.

A more systematic way to get feedback from observers is to use a pilot checklist. Checklists help the design team to focus the feedback and expedite analysis. The following are components that might be included in a pilot checklist.

Design

____ Amount of material appropriate for time

____ Task analysis sufficient

____ Objectives clear and complete

____ All terms properly defined

____ Important content properly stressed

____ Evaluations sufficient

____ Objectives met

Lesson

_____ Directions to learners clear and complete

_____ Pace adequate

_____ Overview adequate

_____ Sequence logical

_____ Benefits to learners explained in enough detail

_____ Links to previous training established where necessary

_____ Content relevant to learners' situation

_____ Transitions comfortable

_____ Reviews adequate

Presentation, Application, Feedback

_____ Media appropriate and effective

_____ Visuals used where possible

_____ Reading level appropriate for learners

_____ Participation adequate

_____ Atmosphere conducive to learning

_____ Presentation methods effective and timely

_____ Applications implemented where needed and for proper time

_____ Checks for understanding implemented where needed and
for proper time

_____ Feedback to learners sufficient

Comments

_____ General comments:

_____ Design comments:

_____ Lesson comments:

_____ Presentation, application, feedback comments:

(This list has been adapted from George M. Piskurich's *Rapid Instructional Design: Learning ID Fast and Right* [Jossey-Bass/Pfeiffer, 2000].)

Learners

Request that the pilot learners participate just as they would if they were in the actual workshop. This includes doing the application exercises, filling out worksheets, and completing the evaluations. After the workshop, the class can be turned into a focus group to offer commentary that the designer might not have gotten otherwise. If the designer is gutsy enough and if the client is sufficiently invested in the workshop, the client could either participate in the pilot as a learner or join the observer group.

Reaction Evaluation

During the pilot and the first offerings of a particular workshop, the designer might use a reaction evaluation at the end of the workshop that assesses learner reactions. These evaluations allow the designer to ask such questions as:

Did learners find the workshop to be interesting?

How was the pacing?

Was it applicable to their needs?

Was there too much content? Too little?

This evaluation is a useful way to assess whether or not the design is on track according to the learners. Review step 9 for a fuller explanation of this type of evaluation.

Learning Evaluation

In addition to the reaction evaluation, the designer may also have developed a performance or a knowledge test to assess whether or not the objectives of the workshop have been met. To review the use of learning evaluations for formative feedback, see step 9.

Worksheets for Applications and Checks for Understanding

Although normally the instructor may not actually be collecting any written applications or checks for understanding, it is very helpful to do so during the pilot. The designer should notice if the directions have been followed and if there are any patterns of incorrect responses.

Debriefing with Client and Learners

Arrange for the pilot learners to stay after the pilot for a debriefing meeting. Include the client if possible. The following are sample focus group questions designed for first-year college students.

Introduce yourself and tell us what course you are here for and a little about the research paper or the speech that you're working on for that course.

What was one thing you really liked about the workshop?

What's one thing you really didn't like about the workshop?

If you had to sit down right now and do the research for your paper, what do you think you could do now that you couldn't do when you walked into the workshop?

What is still confusing?

Let's go through the workshop module by module and get your feedback.

> *For each module, ask:*
>> What worked?
>>
>> What was confusing?
>>
>> What's missing?
>>
>> *You may need to remind students about each module by showing the worksheets and reviewing what they did.*

What was missing from the workshop?

Is there another way you'd prefer to learn about this without coming to the workshop?

There are a few specific things we could use feedback on:

> What do you think are particularly good days and times to schedule these workshops?
>
> What days and times should we avoid?

In closing, do you think this workshop was worth your time or not? Why?

SUMMARY

For some designers, it can be risky teaching brand-new content or choosing a teaching method that they have never used before. Knowing that you will be conducting a pilot workshop can provide the peace of mind to go ahead and try something new.

There are different kinds of pilots, ranging from full-fledged ones with representative learners to ones that simply use the first offering of the workshop as a pilot. Evaluations, post-workshop focus groups, and the use of pilot checklists provide important feedback on the performance of the pilot.

Case Study

The Unravel design team first piloted the workshops with new student library assistants going through their initial library training. Several of the design team members hovered over their draft scripts in the back of the classroom during the pilot. They were looking for things like inconsistencies with the script, difficult transitions in the script, apparent trouble with completion of the application, the need for additional visuals or handout materials, and improvements on worksheets. These observers also captured things the instructor said that were not in the script, but should be.

At the end of the delivery of the workshop, the pilot learners filled out a reaction evaluation that included feedback on their perceptions of the pacing of the workshop, the amount and difficulty of the content, their satisfaction with the amount of presentation and application, and their rating of the handouts.

After this, the pilot group stayed to discuss each segment of the workshop. A facilitator walked the pilot learners through the main modules of the workshop and asked what they liked about it, what they did not like, and how the modules could be improved.

Are You All Set?

Have you

- ✔ Decided on the kind of pilot workshop you will run: external, internal, or "pseudo"?
- ✔ Found ways to entice learners to attend the pilot?
- ✔ Invited observers to help critique the pilot?
- ✔ Had focus groups with the pilot learners and the client after the workshop if possible?
- ✔ Gathered the feedback from the learners, observers, and client along with evaluation data and worksheet results?
- ✔ Used a pilot checklist to organize the feedback?

STEP 17

Change Workshop as Needed

The pilot gives the instructional designer valuable feedback about the workshop design. Reactions to the pilot from the designer, observers, and participants can immediately point out what components are working well and shouldn't be changed. Conversely, they can reveal what components are problematic and need to be redesigned. In addition, the learner assessment data provides further insights into what is working and what is not. Given all the pilot data that can be analyzed, the instructional designer has two decisions to make:

> How much time, resources, and energy will be put into an analysis of the pilot?

> How much time, energy, and resources will be put into a redesign of the workshop?

PILOT ANALYSIS

The first question listed above explores the extent to which the design team will analyze the pilot data. A pilot analysis can be done quickly and at a cursory level, or it can be conducted in a much more systematic way using a data-driven process.

Expedited Pilot Assessment

This choice works for the instructional designer who does not have the time or resources to input data and conduct a formal analysis. In this case the designer would schedule a follow-up design meeting right after the pilot, while verbal feedback is still viable. At this meeting, spread out the assessments and worksheets and look for trends. What seems to be problematic? Look at the script, worksheets, handouts, visuals, assessment tools, and the teaching methods for each presentation, application, and feedback phase of each module.

Have the designer or observers weigh in with their insights to both the pilot they observed and the assessments and worksheets in front of them. Did any of the teaching methods seem to fail? Were the worksheets clear? Does it appear from the assessment and worksheets that the participants in general met the objectives for the workshop? If not, what seems to be the problem?

Data-Driven Pilot Assessment

For design teams that have the resources to have transcripts or notes written out from the pilot and have data from the written materials keyed in and analyzed, a data-driven pilot assessment is invaluable. Data from the assessments can be converted into charts and tables to make analysis easier. This can act as a performance benchmark against which any revisions can be compared. Feedback from the pilot participants can be typed up and grouped under common themes.

This data should then be mapped to each corresponding workshop module. This will allow the design team to tackle the issues one module at a time.

PRIORITIZING CHANGES

There might be many components of a workshop that need changing. The worksheets, for example, may need more work or a presentation teaching method changed. Some changes may be easy, and others might take a considerable amount of time and energy. The designer will have to consider whether or not the additional time and energy are merited.

One way to help with this decision is to try using a decision matrix for prioritizing changes. Think about each component of the workshop and assess how problematic the pilot revealed that component to be. Will the component, if not fixed, impede the learners' capacity to meet the objectives? If so, that component would be considered "highly problematic" on a decision matrix.

Next think about how easily the changes might be made. Is this something that can be done in a short period of time with little effort, or will it mean going back to the drawing board and rethinking an entire teaching method or task? These changes are respectively labeled "easy to change" and "difficult to change" on a decision matrix.

Using the decision matrix (figure 17-1), apply a number to each component of your workshop in the sample form provided below. So, for example, if the worksheets for module 1 are easy to change but are not very problematic, that item would get a 3 and might be put on the back burner for now. Components that are rated 1 or 2 would be addressed first. Items that are rated 3 or 4 could be put on hold and reevaluated after the workshop has been officially delivered. Remember, however, that this matrix is merely a way to discuss prioritization, and not the final word. The designer, for example, may in the end decide that all of the easy fixes would be made first and the more difficult ones would fall below, as shown on the components priority list (figure 17-2). In this case, simply change the sequence of the numbers in the matrix so that they run vertically and not horizontally.

FIGURE 17-1 Decision matrix

	Easy to change	Difficult to change
Highly problematic	1	2
Less problematic	3	4

FIGURE 17-2 Component priority list

Component of Workshop	Score from Decision Matrix
Overall script (includes introduction, transitions, and script format)	
Overall visuals	
Overall handouts	
Overall worksheets	
Reaction evaluation (did it provide useful information or does it need to be changed?)	
Learning evaluation (are the questions problematic?)	
Module 1 presentation	
Module 1 application	
Module 1 feedback	
Module 1 script	
Module 1 visuals	
Module 1 handouts	
Module 1 worksheets	
Continue for all modules. Designers may also apply scores to the worksheets, handouts, visuals, and script that apply to a particular module.	

Case Study

At this point in the design process, the Unravel team was very pressed for time. The fall semester was just around the corner, the team members were busy with other work, and our main goal became the delivery of the workshop, even with some flaws. Because of this, the design team chose the expedited approach to analyze pilot data. Although cursory, this approach gave the team a good deal of useful feedback and some quick ideas for improvements which were implemented immediately.

What emerged most clearly for the design team was that the scripted transitions between modules and between segments within a module were either nonexistent or inadequate. Although the design team had a loose understanding of what these transitions might be, they had never been thought out and scripted. A new instructor given that version of the script would have been lost. The design team decided that this work would make a difference in how successful new instructors would be in working with the script, and that it was worth the design team's time to work on that during this step.

The pilot workshop also revealed the challenges of using the teaching method we chose for the module on "what is the catalog" that was discussed in the chapter on teaching methods (step 12). In this module the instructor used various mail-order catalogs to draw parallels to the library catalog. But the pilot learners were lukewarm about this module. Some felt that it was like kindergarten, while others thought it worked pretty well. The instructor, however, had to work very hard to engage students with this technique. The design team began to have doubts about this approach. Not quite ready to ditch it, however, the design team decided to try it for a full semester before making the final decision.

In the end it was the instructors who decided to put it to final rest. Some who were particularly strong with student interaction could pull it off, but for others the technique was painfully difficult.

Ultimately, the pilot workshop gave the design team confidence in the PAF Model. Pilot learners expressed relief that the workshop wasn't all "boring lecture." Reaction evaluations revealed that the workshop was paced well and that the frequent applications were welcomed. Many participants were surprised at how much they did learn, even though it was just a pilot.

Are You All Set?

Have you

- ✔ Decided how much time, energy, and resources you will put into the pilot analysis?
- ✔ Reviewed the pilot data?
- ✔ Gone through the workshop module by module and identified problems?
- ✔ Prioritized the problems?
- ✔ Identified solutions?
- ✔ Applied those solutions?

STEP 18

Deliver Workshop

The training industry has long realized that those who create their workshops do not necessarily have the skills and interest to teach them. And likewise, those who are skillful and motivated while standing in front of a class do not always enjoy designing its curriculum. Because of this, the role of instructional designer is often a different role than that of an instructor.

Libraries, on the other hand, do not tend to separate these jobs. The instructional designer and the instructor are typically one and the same. This chapter addresses both situations: when the instructional designer is also the instructor and when the instructor is not the instructional designer. Then it will provide an overview of what it means to be a highly effective workshop instructor.

INSTRUCTIONAL DESIGNER AS INSTRUCTOR

The instructional designers who become instructors have a clear advantage. They are intimately connected to the lesson plan. They know exactly why every objective, teaching point, and teaching method was chosen. If an aspect of the lesson plan is not working, they can quickly make alterations while staying true to the original intent of the workshop design. And if they vary from the lesson plan, they realize the implications and can get back on course if they feel it is necessary. This scenario sounds ideal if the instructional designer also happens to be a good instructor.

Some people are naturally good instructors. They can get up in front of a class and command attention, keeping learners focused and engaged. They are the librarians always in demand for teaching. If that is a description of you, go ahead and skip the section on great instruction below. If, however, you just thought, "I wish," keep reading.

NON-DESIGNER AS INSTRUCTOR

Designing workshops and scripting them as covered in this book allows libraries to divide the relationship between instructor and designer and distribute these responsibilities separately. This can mean several things:

> The experienced librarian, who is burnt out on teaching but takes on instructional design responsibilities, can still be the intellectual force behind a workshop without having to teach it.
>
> The outgoing, motivated librarian who enjoys being in front of a class but dislikes designing workshops can be highly effective while using already established lesson plans.
>
> Small staff-training departments can bring their experience to bear by carefully designing workshops and then training others in the library to deliver these workshops in their own units.

A variation of the "non-designer as instructor" theme is when the instructional designer is one of many instructors of the workshop. In either case, what is common is that others who did not design the workshop end up teaching it.

Training the Non-Designer Instructor

When the designer passes a lesson plan to an instructor who has not been involved in the design, some kind of training plan should be in place to make sure that the instructor will successfully deliver the workshop *as designed*.

Why Train?

Without training:

> Instructors may begin "customizing" the lesson plan until finally it is hardly recognizable to the instructional designer.
>
> Instructors who do not understand the importance of the PAF Model for increasing learning may skimp on application and feedback and lengthen the presentation segments.
>
> Instructors who do not understand learner overload may add their own personal teaching points and need-to-knows, thinking they are doing the learners a favor while actually decreasing overall learning.

Training Components

The training of instructors who have not taken part in the design process may include several elements.

Overview of Learning Theory

How do people learn? What gets in the way of learning? How much presentation, application, and feedback do learners need to learn best? An understanding of some basic learning theory helps make sense of the PAF Model used throughout the lesson plan. To train someone in basic learning theory, try using:

Training from a train-the-trainer consultant or company such as Langevin Learning Services

Training from the "center for teaching and learning" (or equivalent) if on a campus

Readings; use step 12 in this book or assign readings from Harold D. Stolovitch and Erica J. Keeps's book *Telling Ain't Training* (ASTD, 2002) or Tony Buzan's book *Use Both Sides of Your Brain* (Bloom, 1991)

> *Sometimes several weeks will pass between classes I teach. Before a class I find it helpful to go through the examples used in the lesson plan and handouts on my own—searching the indexes and catalogs, checking the results. Databases are being constantly updated. By doing a quick search I'm better prepared for the class and can focus on moving the teaching forward, instead of worrying about results I didn't expect.*
>
> —Julia Kiple, Stack Services, University of Minnesota Libraries–Twin Cities

Overview of the Workshop Design

The instructional designer would walk the instructor through the steps of the design process in a very condensed way, starting with needs assessment and going all the way through to the analysis of the pilot and the subsequent changes made. The objective is to communicate the purpose of each component of the lesson plan and script. Although the instructor may be tempted to change the lesson plan somewhere down the line, the instructor needs to understand that there will be trade-offs for doing this.

Skills Training in Workshop Delivery

Gaining competencies in delivery of the lesson plan is the final phase in preparing to teach the workshop. Try using:

Training from a train-the-trainer consultant or company such as Langevin Learning Services

Training from the center for teaching and learning (or equivalent) if on a campus

Readings; use the section below or books such as C. Leslie Charles and Chris Clarke-Epstein's *The Instant Trainer* (McGraw-Hill, 1997) and the chapter "Better Teaching Behaviors" in Trudi Jacobson and Lijuan Xu's *Motivating Students in Information Literacy Classes* (Neal-Schuman, 2004)

BECOMING A GREAT INSTRUCTOR

Being a great instructor is not about you. It's not about how funny you are, how glib or eloquent. Ultimately, it's about how well your learners are learning. By following the PAF Model, the instructor's primary role becomes that of a facilitator of learning. In other words, the instructor becomes the so-called Guide on the Side and not the Sage on the Stage.

This role takes some of the focus and pressure off the instructor. Great instructors, therefore, are actually more like great facilitators. Moving from good to great may be a matter of developing some new habits or dropping some old ones.

Assessing Instructional Abilities

Try It Out

Where do you think you fall on the following scale?

Tip

The four levels in this scale are commonly used stages in the training literature. For a description of how these stages are used to explain training resistance in the library field, see Anne Grodzins Lipow's article "Why Training Doesn't Stick: Who Is to Blame?" in *Library Trends* 38, no. 1 (Summer 1989): 62–72.

Level 1	Level 2	Level 3	Level 4
Unconscious Incompetence	*Conscious Incompetence*	*Conscious Competence*	*Unconscious Competence*
You don't have any idea what it means to be a great instructor or why you should care about improving your skills in this area.	You are aware enough to know that other people are great instructors and that you aren't.	You've learned some skills and put them into practice. However, you must still pay lots of attention to your delivery, and you only have spotty application of instruction skills. Most people will fall into this category.	You have made a habit of practicing a wide range of instruction skills and do so without having to think about them.

Because you are reading this book, chances are you fall in one of the last two columns of the scale. Some of your colleagues who end up teaching your workshop may, however, only be at levels 1 or 2. Assessing your own level and the levels of your instructor colleagues may help you craft an appropriate train-the-trainer plan.

Instructional Skills Assessment

Next we need to spend some time identifying just what it means to be a great instructor and how to assess the gap between these skills and the current skills of the instructor.

The Association of College and Research Libraries' Instruction Section provides some help. It identifies a wide set of core competencies for library instructors, some of which apply to delivery of instruction. These competencies include the ability to "deliver lectures, vary pace and tone, use eye contact, use appropriate gestures, stimulate discussion, and give clear, logical instructions" (from

"Instruction Librarians: Acquiring the Proficiencies Critical to Their Work," in *College & Research Libraries* 54 [March 1993]: 137–49). Many libraries have already worked out similar competencies which are used to assess new or incoming instruction librarians. (If your library does not, the next section in this chapter is on competencies for effective instruction.)

Library-sanctioned core competencies communicate to library instructors what instructional skills are most important for them to have. The next step would be to have a supervisor, head of training or user education, or a trusted colleague use the competencies to assess an instructor's current skill levels and work with the instructor on a development plan. Alternatively, some libraries have access to services like centers for learning, a staff training unit, or at least one skilled and motivated instructor who might be enlisted to help with an instructor assessment and the creation of a development plan.

One possible component of this kind of instructor assessment merits some discussion: the videotaping of the instructor teaching a class. Just the mention of this sends a chill down many a spine. Adding a video component to an instructor's assessment can clearly be a frightening prospect. But this fear needs to be

It's easy ... really!

weighed against its value. Until instructors see such things as their habit of wringing their hands, of inserting "uh's" in every sentence, or of rocking back and forth, they may not feel much motivation to change these behaviors. Be careful, however; videotaping a new instructor can be not just frightening, but a traumatic experience. Making them watch the video can be even worse. A wiser decision might be to save this technique for instructors who have moved into the last two levels of competence shown in the chart above. Start the new instructor with a "mere" observation session and spare them the trauma of the video.

Some Competencies for Delivering Instruction

For those libraries that have not yet identified core competencies for delivering instruction, the following might serve as a stand-in until the library is able to adopt its own competencies for instructional delivery.

Good instructors

- Speak clearly and have well-paced speech
- Avoid speech fillers
- Vary the tone, volume, and rhythm of their speech
- Create a warm, friendly, relaxed atmosphere
- Hold attention
- Show enthusiasm
- Respond to learners' signs of difficulty
- Ask clear questions
- Answer questions well
- Give clear, logical instructions
- Encourage participation
- Stimulate discussion

> ### Tip
>
> Use this list (or a list like it) to create an instructor's evaluation form that can be used during in-class evaluations. Next to each competency could be a Likert Scale with the degree of competence the instructor exhibits and a place for comments. (A Likert Scale is usually a numerical scale from 1–7, 1–6, or 1–5, with 1 being the low score and 5, 6, or 7 being the high score.)

If the competency list is not used in a concrete way, it risks being worked on, sweated over, and then merely filed away. By creating opportunities for instructors to be assessed by their peers, supervisors, or by specialists in training and education, your competency list can become a vital part of training and evaluating library instructors.

Advice for Delivering a Great Workshop

Here are some tips for delivering an effective, high-quality workshop.

Evaluate everything

Create opportunities for supervisors or colleagues to give you feedback. Study reaction evaluation feedback from the learners. Ask learners or clients for candid feedback. Ask yourself, "What could I do next time to make my teaching even more effective?"

Get trained

Take a train-the-trainer course, an acting course, or periodically read up on instruction skills.

Partner with the instructional designer

The instructor is in a great position to note problems and identify possible improvements to the instructional design. The instructor can then become part of the instructional design team for future revisions of the workshop.

Learn something entirely new

Every once in a while, learn something entirely new to you. This will remind you what it is like to be a beginner who gets quickly overloaded, confused, and frustrated, and it will keep you sensitive to what your learners might be experiencing.

Within the Workshop

Begin before the beginning

Learners will begin to judge whether or not the workshop is worth their time from the very beginning. Is the room set up? Are handouts distributed already? Do you as instructor greet the learners and make them feel welcome? Is there a sense of liveliness and interest created in the room, perhaps through colorful visuals in view or music playing in the background?

Move around

Take advantage of all the space in the room. Vary where you stand during the workshop, so that by the end you have spent time leading the workshop from the front, each side, and from the back. This makes learners change focus, move around, and take their eyes off the computer monitors (if applicable).

Modulate your tone

Speak loudly to emphasize important points. Be dramatic to draw attention, and speak softly as a contrast. Pause for contrast. Change the speed and tempo of your speaking. Make noises to add to your voice modulation. Slap your hand against the flipchart, or tap your marker against the white board.

Make eye contact and smile

Look every single person in the room right in the eyes as frequently as you can. Have a conversation; do not talk *at* the learners. Smile more than frown.

Get out of the spotlight

> The less you dominate, the more participation will happen. When the spotlight is off you, try sitting down to minimize your dominance in the class.

Mix it up

> If it's possible to do so given the lesson plan, switch around the modules so that the workshop is a little different. For even more variety, trade in a newly designed module that teaches the same objectives as the old one.

Advice for Delivering Someone Else's Workshop Design

Although there can be many benefits in handing over a design to a trained and enthusiastic library instructor, there can also be some compelling challenges. Here is some advice for the non-designer instructor to help make the process go more smoothly and successfully.

Rework the script

> Get hold of the script in electronic format and reformat it to suit you. This means highlighting headers, writing in notes, and making it feel like your own. This does not mean changing any part of the design (such as content or methods).

Pilot the script

> Don't just do a mental rehearsal. Find a group of library assistants, volunteers, or students who need training in the content you are teaching and have a practice run-through with them. If this isn't possible, enlist a friendly colleague or two to sit in on a practice class.

Know the script

> No one wants to be read to from a script. Make sure that you know it well enough to follow it without reading every word.

Check your timing

> Keep a digital clock in a place where you can see it and make sure the script is marked with start and end times for each component of the lesson plan.

Focus on the learners

> After all the preparation, you should be able to make the focus of your workshop the learners, and not the script. Think of yourself as having a conversation with the learners.

Relax

> You're dealing with a great lesson plan. If a few things go badly, chances are the learners will still achieve at least some of the objectives. So take a breath, relax, and move on.

Pause

It's not a race. Although it can feel like the goal is to get through the script, the learners are trying to understand it for the first time. Pause between sentences and segments. Pause after asking a question. Slow down the pace of your speaking and enunciate.

LEARN MORE

If you are interested in learning more about great delivery, there are many great books and resources out there. A few suggestions include:

Tony Jeary's lively advice in *Life Is a Series of Presentations: 8 Ways to Punch Up Your People Skills at Work, at Home, Anytime, Anywhere* (Simon and Schuster, 2004).

Robert Pike has a great chapter on presentation techniques, preparation, and a lot more of interest in *Creative Training Techniques Handbook: Tips, Tactics, and How-To's for Delivering Effective Training* (Lakewood, 1992).

Get hold of some training videos for trainers. One designed for speakers is *Public Speaking: Time to Stand* (Films for the Humanities and Sciences, 2000). Skip ahead to the sections on public speaking.

To see what training opportunities are available at a local level, check out the following organizations.

American Society for Training and Development (ASTD), at http://www.astd.org

International Association of Presentation Professionals, at http://www.iapp.org

National Speakers Association, at http://www.nsaspeaker.org

The Speakers Roundtable, at http://www.speakersroundtable.com

Toastmasters International, at http://www.toastmasters.org

SUMMARY

Poor delivery of a workshop can negatively impact its effectiveness even if the workshop is designed particularly well. Identifying expectations of instructor competencies, assessing these competencies, and creating a development plan for instructors can make a big difference in ensuring that a workshop is well delivered.

At the University of Minnesota Libraries, the Unravel design team is made up of six or seven individuals. Although all of these people teach the workshops, over twice as many instructors are recruited from the library at large. They come from all different areas and have very different ranks and levels of experience.

Case Study

In order to bring everyone up to a certain level of competence, volunteer instructors go through a three-part training sequence to prepare for instructing the Unravel workshops.

Part one is a one-hour presentation on the design of the workshop. The presenter walks the trainees through an overview of the entire design process so they understand who the learners are, what their needs are, and exactly why every piece of the lesson plan was designed the way it was.

Part two consists of each trainee observing a workshop led by one of the design team members.

Part three consists of each trainee assisting a veteran Unravel instructor or one of the design team members who teaches the workshop. Depending on the trainee's confidence and past experience as an instructor, she may choose to assist in several more workshops, perhaps teaching only one or two modules of the workshop at a time. Eventually, the trainee will graduate to become a lead instructor.

Although this training process is actually asking a lot from the "volunteer" Unravel instructors, there are several additional components that would really make this an effective training process:

Training in effective presentation and facilitation skills

Follow-up assessment to give instructors ongoing feedback about what is working and what needs changing

What we are finding is that without these added components, we have less "quality control" over the workshops. It is also easier for the veteran Unravel instructors to slowly move further away from the original design intent if there are no official checks on them in the way of ongoing instructor assessments.

Are You All Set?

Have you

✔ Decided who will teach the workshop—the instructional designers, the instructors, or both?

✔ Identified what it means to be a great instructor and created instructional competencies to this end?

✔ Assessed your own—or the instructor's—instructional competencies?

✔ Trained the instructors to teach the workshop?

✔ Delivered the workshop?

Evaluate Workshop

At this point in the process the workshop has been designed, piloted, and delivered. The tools for assessing learning that were developed in step 9 have given the designer a body of data on how well the workshop design ultimately performed. Did the learners value the workshop? Did they learn what they needed to learn? Did it make an impact on their library-related project or goal? Did it ultimately make the learners more successful?

Recall Kirkpatrick's four levels of evaluation covered in step 9:

Level 1: Reaction evaluation

Asks: Did they *like* it?

Level 2: Learning evaluation

Asks: Did they *get* it?

Level 3: Behavioral evaluation

Asks: Do they *apply* it?

Level 4: Results evaluation

Asks: Did it make a *difference*?

This chapter will break down the analysis process for each level.

LEVEL 1: REACTION EVALUATIONS

Reaction evaluations provide the designer with feedback about what the learners liked and didn't like about the workshop. Questions that reveal such things as pacing (too fast, too slow) or organization (too rigid, too flexible) can help get the design back on track. Questions that have the learners identify the expectations they felt weren't met or what they are still confused about can help point out design flaws to be dealt with in subsequent iterations of the workshop design.

This kind of feedback is helpful, but is knowing that 20 percent of the participants feel the workshop is too slow, for example, meaningful enough? How about 40 percent of them? 60 percent? Does this mean the workshop pacing is unsatisfactory? What numbers mean the design is successful, and what numbers mean it's not measuring up?

To make the results of reaction feedback meaningful, the designer can do several things:

Set the data from the pilot workshop as a baseline performance standard. If evaluations from the revised workshop design exceed the baseline performance standard, that aspect of the workshop would be considered successful.

Set a performance standard as a goal. So, for example, one could say that if 80 percent of the learners were satisfied or extremely satisfied with the workshop, the workshop design has met a goal.

Identify a performance standard from other workshops that have been deemed successful by the client or the library. Compare your current workshop results with this standard.

If the standard or standards are not met, the designer would then have the data to make an informed decision about whether or not a redesign process was warranted.

LEVEL 2: LEARNING EVALUATIONS

Level-2 evaluations assess whether or not the learners actually learned what the designer wanted them to learn. Sometimes these evaluations are knowledge-based (multiple-choice questions, fill-in-the-blank questions, etc.) tests, and sometimes they are performance tests (complete x task). They have the potential to provide rich feedback to the designer as to where the design is weak, and summative feedback that the designer can use to market future offerings of the workshop and in performance evaluations.

Feedback to Designer

Performance tests that ask learners to complete a task can provide ample feedback to the designer as to how successful the design is. If the performance test is observed by the designer or instructor and if the learners are asked to discuss their process while doing it, exact problems can be pinpointed.

Do most learners seem to be missing the distinction between an index and a catalog, for example? Or are they still trying to type in the title of the article in the catalog to see if it is owned by the library? If errors like these become patterned responses, the designer can zero in on the weak area of the instructional design.

The next best kind of performance test for feedback would be those that include a research journal. Here the learners are instructed to document their performance process. If there seems to be a patterned error in certain areas, the designer will know where to focus a redesign.

Knowledge test questions are also useful, especially when mapped back to workshop modules. Any consistently incorrect test result is a red flag to the designer calling for some level of redesign.

Summative Feedback about the Workshop

Learning evaluations can be analyzed in the aggregate. Look at how well overall the learners do on these evaluations and set performance standards for these numbers. For example, if most students get As on the knowledge test, but some fail, is that satisfactory to the designer? If only a few get As and most get Cs, is that good enough? As in level-1 reaction evaluations, the designer needs to figure out the criteria for deeming the workshop a success.

- The designer could administer a pretest to establish a performance or knowledge baseline.
- The designer could identify a standard to which he or she decides to aspire. For example, one standard might be that if a learner is able to complete 80 percent of the performance or knowledge evaluations correctly, the workshop is deemed successful and subsequent redesigns are put on hold.
- The designer could use a standard from a similar test from another workshop for comparison to see if there was improvement.

This assessment can be done on a test-by-test level, but it is even more helpful to break down the data to the module level. Since each question is mapped to a module through a specific objective and teaching point, learning evaluations will reveal how successful each module is.

This data can be used in multiple ways: in promotional materials for future workshops, in accountability documentation at the library level, and in individual performance evaluations.

LEVEL 3: BEHAVIORAL EVALUATIONS

Level-3 evaluations seek to discover if learners actually applied their learning in "the real world." As described in step 9, grading rubrics are a common way to systematically evaluate behavioral changes. Setting performance standards as was done with level-1 and level-2 evaluations helps make the results of behavioral evaluations meaningful.

If the results are positive, they provide the client, the designers, and the library with powerful data that can be used to build the library's reputation as an effective educator and instill confidence in current and future clients.

But what about disappointing behavioral evaluations? Surprisingly, these can be just as powerful. Most librarians know that the one-shot workshop is inadequate at best to make a substantive impact on information literacy, but this does not mean that our greater community (such as our school, college, or district) knows this. Disappointing behavioral results coupled with strong level-1 and level-2 evaluations may be leveraged into an argument for an actual *information literacy* program that goes beyond one-shot training workshops. This kind of program might be more extensive, more embedded into the client's programs, and more recognized as an important contribution.

A Word of Caution

Moving from level-2 to level-3 evaluation challenges the designer's ability to identify whether or not it was the workshop in question that caused a learner to perform well or poorly. Perhaps the learner received help from a family member or friend, got help at the reference desk, or came with prior knowledge. Controlling these variables would be extremely difficult and time-consuming, and a "simple" pre-evaluation is probably not going to be feasible. Most likely the best a design team can do is state in the analysis that there may be other factors that affected improved performance, and to include their assumptions or reasons for why they think the workshop was the main driver of improvement.

LEVEL 4: RESULTS EVALUATIONS

This is the boldest level of evaluation. It tries to get to the heart of the matter: did the workshop make any overall difference in the success of the learners? The measures for this will be as different as the learners and clients are different:

In a sales company, did sales numbers go up?

In a service, did customer service improve?

At a college, did first year retention numbers increase?

In secondary school, did a greater number of students go on to compete regionally in programs like History Day?

Compare the numbers from before and after the workshop. If possible, couple this data with reaction data from level 1 that says that learners themselves think the workshop made a difference (in sales, customer service, retention, grades, etc.). Combining data from other evaluations is especially important with level-4 evaluations, since the cautionary note above applies manyfold to this evaluation level.

SUMMARY

There are four main types of evaluation tools: reaction evaluations, learning evaluations, behavioral evaluations, and results evaluations. The designer uses various techniques to identify performance standards for each of the evaluation tools used. These standards are measured against the actual performance of the workshop. Underperforming aspects of the workshop can then be prioritized for redesign. Positive data from the evaluations can be used to prove the effectiveness and importance of library workshops to the client, the library administration, and the larger community.

The Unravel design team at the University of Minnesota Libraries started with level-1 and level-2 evaluations of its workshops. These were manageable levels that the library could administer without too much work and that would provide important formative data.

Workshop pilots all started with a level-1 reaction evaluation with the pilot group and were continued with the actual workshop participants. Evaluation feedback from Unravel 1: Orientation and Tour was particularly interesting to the design team, since several members of the group were unconvinced that the tour component would be well received. Did the learners think it was a waste of time? Would they recommend it to their friends? The findings showed that yes, the students valued the tour and wanted us to keep it.

Examining level-1 feedback in graph format was useful. Figure 19-1 is a chart for the Unravel 2 workshop from the fall of 2001 summarizing responses to the statement, "This session completely met my expectations." On the left (y) axis are the number of responses (out of 235), and along the bottom is a Likert Scale from 1 to 7, with 1 being low and 7 being high. This shows that the majority of participants felt that the session met or exceeded their expectations.

Case Study

FIGURE 19-1   Unravel 2 workshop level 1 feedback

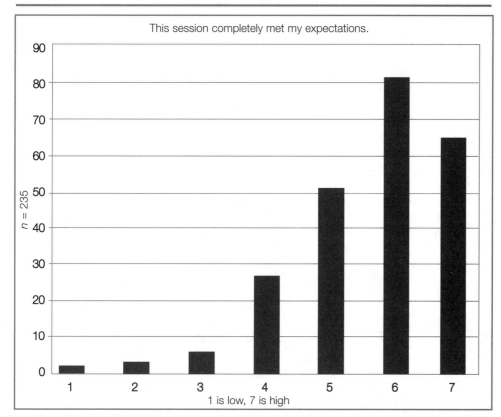

Level-2 learning evaluation data caused the team great concern, however. Figure 19-2 shows the responses to eight multiple-choice questions on a brief test administered at the end of the workshop. The shaded boxes indicate what should have been the correct answer. The team was shooting for a correct choice of 80 percent or better for each question. Questions 2, 3, and 5 are the problem areas:

Question 2

Searching in _____ will give you a list of articles that have been published on your topic.

      a. an article index
      b. MNCAT
      c. a library catalog
      d. the Assignment Calculator

Question 3

A good starting place to search for articles on your topic is in _____.

      a. subject headings
      b. MNCAT
      c. Expanded Academic Index
      d. a library catalog

Question 5

To find out if the University of Minnesota Libraries own the article you want, you need to search by the _____ in MNCAT.

      a. title of the article
      b. title of the journal/magazine/newspaper
      c. author of the article
      d. any of these

This data pointed to a major problem area of the workshop—the module that covered MNCAT (the library OPAC). We were clearly unsuccessful at helping students grasp the difference between MNCAT and the article indexes. We also could not seem to get through to them that MNCAT has only the periodical records and not citations or the full text of articles.

FIGURE 19-2   **Unravel 2 workshop level 2 evaluation data**

Answer Chosen	Question 1	Question 2	Question 3	Question 4	Question 5	Question 6	Question 7	Question 8
A	2%	73%	7%	2%	2%	4%	8%	8%
B	83%	21%	23%	91%	72%	4%	5%	6%
C	11%	4%	66%	5%	1%	89%	2%	81%
D	4%	2%	3%	1%	24%	2%	84%	1%
No Answer	0	0	1%	1%	1%	1%	1%	4%

After examining this feedback, the team tried numerous remedies—graphics, a Powerpoint, and reinforcement of the teaching point throughout the module. To our dismay, however, test scores have not noticeably improved. The mental models of the students are so foreign to these concepts that we have finally implemented a technological solution that fits better with the current research mental model—a federated search engine. This struggle illustrates that if you can't change the user, try changing the technology or the process.

Are You All Set?

Have you

- ✔ Crunched the numbers from all the evaluation tools?
- ✔ Separated out the data by module?
- ✔ Created baseline performance standards?
- ✔ Compared these standards to the workshop evaluation data?

Change Workshop

By this point, many hours of development time have been put into the workshop design. If the workshop was piloted and improved (steps 16 and 17), the final product is most likely to be highly effective. Now the instructional designers have a choice: they can either continue to improve the workshop based on the latest evaluation; or they can leave the workshop design as is and use the evaluation analysis at the library and community levels to promote the library's educational efforts.

CHOOSING TO IMPROVE THE WORKSHOP

If the workshop is going to be offered many more times, has high visibility, or had disappointing results in the last evaluation, the designers may decide to continue to work on the design.

This step is basically a repeat of what was done to change the workshop after the pilot. The main differences are that now the designers probably have

A larger body of data upon which to draw

More experience instructing the workshop

Others who may have instructed the workshop who can contribute to the improvements

A group of learners who can be enlisted for focus groups, surveys, or discussions

Improve or Redesign?

Next the design team should think about the extent to which the workshop needs improvement. Does a module just need some tweaking? Should there be a new handout or visual? Then the designers may decide to quickly make some improvements.

If the workshop needs more than just a minor fix, the designers will need to conduct a quick diagnosis of where the design process is failing the learners. The table below can help identify which steps need attention in the redesign process.

If this is the problem . . .	Focus on these steps . . .
Mismatch between what client wants and what is covered	Step 1: Assess needs
Learners report feeling overwhelmed	Step 2: Learner analysis Step 3: Brainstorm content Step 4: Filter the nice-to-knows from the need-to-knows Step 12: Brainstorm teaching methods Step 13: Choose teaching methods
Learners complain about the teaching methods	Step 12: Brainstorm teaching methods Step 13: Choose teaching methods
Learners complain that the content is irrelevant or unimportant	Step 1: Assess needs Step 2: Learner analysis
Learners are underperforming in the checks for understanding, applications, or the learner evaluation	Step 10: Create checks for understanding Step 12: Brainstorm teaching methods Step 13: Choose teaching methods and review effectiveness of the techniques themselves
Instructors are having trouble following the script	Step 14: Structure workshop Step 18: Deliver workshop

Once the design team feels fairly confident the problems are identified, they can back up to the proper step in the design process to correct it. If the change was significant enough, remember to pilot the changes if possible.

SUMMARY

What is good enough? The designer decides at this point in the design process whether it is worth the time and energy to pursue an even better, more effective workshop. There are three choices: making small-scale revisions to pieces of the workshop, launching a large-scale redesign effort on specific modules of the workshop, or completely revamping the entire workshop. Designers can save time by identifying specific problems and linking them to their respective steps in the redesign process.

Case Study

The University of Minnesota's Unravel 2: The Research Process workshop is attended by more than 1,300 students each year. It is the only workshop that is offered at this rate to students and is the linchpin workshop in the Unravel the Library series. Because of this it has undergone the most redesign cycles. In practice this has meant that in any given summer at least one or two modules of the workshop have been either completely changed or improved upon.

One module on keyword searching was completely dropped, but several years later a new one was created in its place. A presentation segment in a module on identifying known items in the OPAC was greatly revised. Even an entire workshop (Unravel for Grads) was put on the chopping block after the design team analyzed the evaluations and the demand for such a workshop. Recently, the design team has had to completely revisit the curriculum due to the procurement of a federated search engine.

In contrast to Unravel 2, the first workshop in the series, Unravel 1: Orientation and Tour, has not undergone nearly as many revisions and hardly any redesigning. This workshop is offered to fewer people, has less lofty objectives, and has garnered above-average evaluations. The design team weighed the benefits and costs of redesigns and decided instead to settle on small revisions to it. These have paid off well, making Unravel 1 the highest return on investment, so to speak.

Are You All Set?

Have you

✔ Chosen the level of changes you want to make to the workshop? Revisions or a redesign?

✔ Identified at which step the biggest problems in the design process might have occurred?

✔ Revisited those steps and made changes?

✔ Piloted these changes if possible?

Final Thoughts

A paradigm is, as Adam Smith says, like water to a fish. It's the way the world looks—the way it is. When one is deep within a paradigm, it's difficult to see another.

Many librarians and staff inhabit a teaching paradigm that is sometimes referred to as the "education paradigm." In this paradigm the job of library instructors is to transmit content to the people sitting in their classrooms. These "content transmitters" are able to pack enormous amounts of information into a short workshop, show numerous databases, and even have time for some unstructured hands-on time at the end. And then their job is done. In other words, they pour, and it's the recipients' responsibility to catch that information, make sense of it, apply it, and learn from it. This paradigm is handy, because then the library instructor can take little (or maybe even no) responsibility for the students being able to apply the content in their real lives. What makes this a paradigm is that for many people it is the water to the fish. It is the way education *is*. "Everybody" knows that because "everybody" grew up being taught in that paradigm. But not so anymore.

In contrast is the paradigm this book takes and the one that more and more teachers, professors, and trainers are taking. In the "performance-based instruction paradigm," the instructor is responsible for increasing learning and performance. Instead of downloading information, the instructor's job is to coach and facilitate learners to master a specific task or come to an understanding about something that they are fully prepared to apply outside of the classroom.

> *It is much more fun to work with a performance-based instruction paradigm than it is to follow the "just pour it on 'em" education paradigm that we all know. It is also more challenging. Once you learn how to engage students in learning, however, the magic begins. Instead of being a distant, somewhat hostile talking head, you become a coach who makes it possible for students to better achieve what they have come to do: conduct good research that will facilitate their success in college.*
>
> —Debra Payne Chaparro, PhD Student and Teaching Assistant, University of Minnesota Libraries–Twin Cities

The challenge can be that some people in the library organization operate within the "education paradigm," while others operate within the "performance-based instruction paradigm." For some, this conflict isn't a problem. But if the person or people who evaluate and reward you operate under the education paradigm, and you operate under the performance-based instruction paradigm, you have a problem.

First, as you have garnered from learning about the instructional design process, performance-based instruction takes time. You can't just throw together some handouts, pull together an outline, and march in with your lecture–demo–hands-on formula. The key to success in this paradigm is a learner-centered approach with a studied, thoughtful preparation process and a careful analysis of evaluation data. The rewards are learners who are actually learning and performing at a higher level and who are succeeding at their goals. The question then becomes: is this what is valued in your library? I don't mean what people in your organization *say* that shows this is valued, but rather what they *do* to value it.

By fighting for even just minor changes in the library, you and your performance-based instruction paradigm colleagues will help to make two things happen: your efforts will be acknowledged and rewarded, and you will begin to shift the library's instruction program from the education paradigm to the performance-based instruction paradigm.

CHANGING PARADIGMS

One of the interesting things about paradigms is they can operate simultaneously. Your library organization already holds multiple paradigms about all kinds of things. These can include, "The longer you are a librarian, the more you get paid," or "If patrons are really having problems with their research, they will seek help at the reference desk," or "We can get better work done if we decentralize and become team-based." So what has this got to do with the performance-based instruction paradigm? The important thing is that once one paradigm starts to change, often others do too.

Look around. Are other paradigms changing? If not in your organization, what about in the larger organization, such as your college or business? What this means is that people are causing other rules to change and creating new games to play in. This is a good sign that bodes well for shifting to the performance-based instruction paradigm.

In order to understand where you might currently be in the shift, it might help to think of your colleagues falling roughly into three categories: the paradigm shifters, the early adopters, and the laggards or late adopters.

Paradigm shifters

Paradigms are often instigated by someone considered an outsider who doesn't fully understand the current paradigm's rules and boundaries.

Because they are outsiders (e.g., new to the field, consultants, without an M.L.S. degree, or people who lurk at the fringe), they don't typically have institutional power behind them.

Give this book to an educational paradigm person and note their strongly negative reaction: "All these steps and all this time for what? To spoon-feed those people? If they don't know enough to want to learn how to do research [or fill in the blank] the right way, why bother?"

Early adopters

The catalysts are the paradigm shifters, but they are soon followed by the early adopters. In this case, the early adopters might be those instruction librarians who have an intuitive sense that the new paradigm will help them be much more effective and build a stronger reputation as educators. This group is convinced that it is worth the time and energy to learn the new skills, build the new knowledge, and change the way they teach.

Laggards or late adopters

After watching and hearing and learning from the current adopters, they are finally convinced that the new paradigm is worth the time and energy to move into it.

So the million-dollar question is, how might you support your laggards and late adopters to move into acceptance of this new paradigm? As much as I would like to now give you a formula for causing a paradigm shift in your organization, the bad news is that this topic is worth a whole other book.

So what you're saying is that maybe we need to start thinking outside of the box.

There are a few classics that I would recommend if you'd like to explore this further:

John Kotter's *Leading Change* (Harvard Business School Press, 1996) is as close to a blueprint for leading a change effort that I have seen. Kotter breaks down the process into eight stages that end in a transformed culture.

Peter Senge, Art Kleiner, and others have gotten together again to write a wonderful book called *The Dance of Change: The Challenges of Sustaining Momentum in Learning Organizations* (Currency/Doubleday, 1999). This book brings theory and practice together into a practical work about organizational transformation.

Joel Arthur Barker's book *Paradigms: The Business of Discovering the Future* (HarperBusiness, 1993) strikes me as Thomas Kuhn (remember him?) for the masses. His book is full of concrete examples of paradigm shifts and the early adopters who make new paradigms a success.

And, of course, the instructional design process itself may very well be a key driver in creating a new performance-based instructional paradigm for several reasons.

The ability to report on a rich body of evaluation data can create valuable outcome measurements for library administrators and turn their attention to more opportunities for instruction that has clear outcomes.

Closer partnerships with clients can be the catalyst to move the one-shot workshop approach into a more substantial and effective educational partnership.

Involving education paradigm librarians and staff in the instructional design might very well convert them one by one.

In parting I wish you great luck! May this endeavor lead to your library taking on even greater educational roles that have higher impact and value to our communities.

Forms and supplementary materials to help you design your next workshop are available at http://www.tc.umn.edu/~jveldof/WorkshopDesign/.

APPENDIX
Step-by-Step Checklist

The instructional design process is often a nonlinear process that can make it difficult to track which steps still need to be done. The following checklist can be used to build a work plan and track completion of each step in the design process. More appendixes are available at

http://www.tc.umn.edu/~jveldof/ WorkshopDesign/

Step	Deadline	Date Completed
Assess needs		
Analyze learners		
Brainstorm content		
Filter content		
Group content into modules		
Create task analysis		
Create teaching points		
Write objectives		
Build evaluation tools		
Create checks for understanding		
Revisit the need-to-knows		
Brainstorm teaching methods		
Choose teaching methods		
Structure workshop		
Develop materials		
Pilot workshop		
Change workshop as needed		
Deliver workshop		
Evaluate workshop		
Change workshop		

Index

Jerilyn Veldof is Director of Undergraduate Initiatives for the University of Minnesota Libraries in the Twin Cities. In this role she leads planning, coordinating, resource development, and campus collaborations with respect to the undergraduate library experience. She was previously Coordinator of User Education, in which she worked to incorporate information literacy into the campus curriculum at the University of Minnesota. Veldof holds a master's degree in library science from the State University of New York at Buffalo. She has led numerous workshops and written more than a half dozen articles and book chapters, primarily in the areas of instructional design, assessment, and usability.